Master/slave Mastery Protocols

Focusing the intent of your relationship

by M. Jen Fairfield
and
Robert J. Rubel, Ph.D.

Other Books
by Robert J. Rubel and M. Jen Fairfield

Books are published by Red Eight Ball Press, Austin, TX. Signed copies are available through www.KinkMastery.com. You can also order through Amazon.

BDSM Mastery—Basics: Your guide to play, parties, and scene protocols
(Book One in the BDSM Mastery Series)

BDSM Mastery—Relationships: a guide for creating mindful relationships for Dominants and submissives
(Book Two in the BDSM Mastery Series)

Master/slave Mastery: Updated handbook of concepts, approaches, and practices
(Book One in the Master/slave Mastery Series)

Master/slave Mastery: Refining the fire—ideas that matter
(Book Two in the Master/slave Mastery Series)

Is THAT what they meant? A book of practical communication insights

Master/slave Mastery Protocols

Focusing the intent of your relationship

by M. Jen Fairfield
and
Robert J. Rubel, Ph.D.

Red Eight Ball Press
P.O. Box 171303
Austin, TX 78717

Red Eight Ball Press
P.O. Box 171303 Austin, TX 78717

Master/slave Mastery—Protocols
Focusing the intent of your relationship

Layout: I particularly wish to recognize and thank slave kitara for the exceptional job she did laying out this book.

Library of Congress catalog card number: 2016949538

Published by Red Eight Ball Press
Printed in the United States of America

Dedication

This book is dedicated to those who live in authority-imbalanced relationships, however you label them.

We're a small group, but we tend to be extremely skilled at maintaining complex relationship structures. I congratulate anyone who is reading this book. I hope you enjoy it.

Structured relationships can lead you down exciting paths or challenging paths. In my experience, as much depends on how much you know about communication and enlight-ened leadership as on willingness. Unenlightened leader-ship often ends in physical or mental abuse; an unwilling (or reluctantly-willing) follower will stymie their partner's best intentions.

Bottom line: it's an unusual path that is filled with opportunities not available to traditional couples following main-stream customs.

We've written this book for those of you who want to put some magic into your relationship. In that light, we hope that this book adds useful tools to your relationship toolbox. That is certainly our intent.

M. Jen Fairfield and Robert Rubel
Austin, Texas
2016

Foreword by Dr. Bob

About Protocols

Writing a Protocol Manual is not primarily about writing rules of service. Writing a Protocol Manual helps you examine and refine your relationship and your relationship management style. The very process of creating a Manual such as this reveals the kinds of service Master *really* wants from the slave and the kinds of service the slave can actually deliver. In that light, writing a Protocol Manual is an exercise in clarifying the intent of your relationship.

Some Masters / Dominants seem to be allergic to the idea of using formal protocols. I've never quite understood that. Let me try to make you less bristly over the word.

A "protocol" is simply an agreed-upon standard that describes how to perform a task. It's not a big deal. For example, you have a certain way of holding your knife and fork in this country that differs somewhat from the way Europeans hold their cutlery. So, US dining protocols are slightly different from European dining protocols. Neither is "better" than the other. Nobody is forcing you to eat in one style or the other, and at that level of detail, your cutlery protocols seldom matter. However, if you're at a fairly formal dinner and those around you are using different cutlery protocols than yours, you'll tend to stand out.

Here's another example. You see flashing red and blue lights in your rear-view mirror. While "getting a ticket" may be a problem, at least you know the standard protocols for dealing with the situation: stay in your car; keep your hands on the steering wheel; be polite to the officer*. In this case, you probably have the intention of not making matters worse; you probably intend to be polite and in control of yourself. I would argue that Master/slave relationships work precisely that way: you have the intention of not creating relationship troubles, being polite to one another, and being in control of yourself.

In your own relationship, I suspect that you use quite a few protocols, but you may not *name them* "protocols." Master probably wants certain foods prepared or presented in a special way, wants to go through some ceremony at bedtime, and cares how you bring their morning coffee. These individual actions (protocols) combine to form the rituals of your life. These everyday actions help focus attention on Master's (and slave's) intent.

Protocols can be your friend. We've written this book to help you recognize protocols for what they are, label them, and use them to your advantage as relationship-bonding tools.

* Ann Goodpet: "Designing Practical Protocols" presentation, 2008.

Biased as I am, I assert that protocols help to reprogram both the Master's and the slave's brains. They help you to create habits. Protocols don't merely define how you look on the outside; protocols help to shape how you think on the inside. Since protocols specify the way Master wants this particular slave to do things, and since people are different from one another, protocol manuals are person-specific.

You can build protocols into any kind of relationship system (M/s, D/s, TPE). They simply clarify each person's role. Done well, protocols serve as a moment-by-moment recognition of the unusual nature of your relationship. They enable you to honor one another continually.

This book is as much about mindset and values as it is about protocols, themselves. This book explains how our protocols grew out of our values. Once you've completed this book, it's up to you to create your own protocols—based on your own mindset and values.

Protocols put the polish on the relationship. In that light, this is a book of relationship polish.

Contents

The Protocol Manual by Jen
Introduction

This is my own protocol manual for my own slave. I'm not trying to win converts or say this should be YOUR protocol manual for YOUR slave. In 2007, my slave, Robert Rubel (also known as Dr. Bob), published *Protocols for the Female slave: Handbook of theory and practice*. At the time, that book was his protocol manual for his slave.

Life takes turns beyond our understanding and control. Improbably, Bob and I found ourselves drawn together as a couple. We started as sexual play partners and transitioned to SM play partners. Since I'd been the dominant partner in my previous marriage, I tried to introduce my usual D/s dynamic into the evolving relationship with Bob. That didn't work; Bob is not submissive.

In 2011 we decided to bring structure into our relationship and were having trouble blending Bob's strict formal Master/slave style with my more casual team approach. By SouthPlains Leather Alliance in 2012 we had still not blended these two concepts, however, Raven Kaldera and

Joshua Tenpenny presented their Team Model of M/s concept, which presented me with additional information to help Bob understand. It took another six months before he began to understand and yet another two years before full understanding occurred.

But, we were having world-class sex and having a lot of fun reveling in the newness of blending such dissimilar lives, so we kept trying to work out a fit. Finally, in the summer of 2014, Bob had a conceptual breakthrough and realized that he could be a "dominant in service." He realized that while D/s relationships rely on one person being a D-type and the other being an s-type, Master/salve relationships were about serving and obeying. He realized he could be a dominant person in a subordinate relationship role and maintain the integrity of and M/s dynamic. He was surprised. He also realized that this was new information in the heterosexual M/s community.

But, I'm getting ahead of myself.

Let me now welcome you to our life.

This book is essentially an autobiographical snapshot of the way we live. Unlike the way Vanillas live, we put a lot of thought into how, exactly, we want things done. Well, let me rephrase that: I've put a lot of thought into how I want things done. Since the rules of our structure give me the authority to require my slave to enrich my life as I wish, this book tells him how to do that.

We're offering this to you in the spirit of sharing. We're sharing what *we* have found helps *us* to make our relationship run smoothly. While it's unlikely that you'll want to live the way we like to live, we hope it will give you some ideas for enriching your own lives.

As already mentioned, while Bob is my slave, he is not a submissive. He is a dominant male who has chosen for his own reasons to serve me from a subordinate position. For readers unfamiliar with us (from our numerous books and lectures), we live in a "CEO/COO" corporate model for our personal Master/slave relationship (A Chief Executive Officer is the overall head of a company; the Chief Operating Officer is responsible for making sure that internal operations are running correctly). I provide the relationship vision; he makes it happen. My job is to keep us on track.

(Note: If you're not familiar with the mechanics of Master/slave relationship structures, you can find our books on that subject on KinkMastery.com.)

Before you start reading, I'd like to admit something. The extensive and detailed discussions Bob and I had to go through to produce this Manual strengthened our relationship. Importantly, it stopped Bob from serving me as he's taught his former slave of eight years. It forced him to take the time to write out how I, personally, wanted to be served.

There was a parallel benefit, too. As Bob's the writer, the process of recording our discussions and organizing them into this Manual helped him quite a bit. He has Asperger

Syndrome and tends to operate out of a "book of life." His behavior and speech changes somewhat depending upon which "book" he thinks he should be using at that time. We'd had some problems in the early years of our relationship because Bob would swing from speaking to me from his dominant "boyfriend" side to a rather icky "submissive slave" side. The voices were completely different.

So: writing all this out helped my slave develop its current self -identity. Of course, what helps him helps our relationship: what helps our relationship clearly helps me.

Preparing this Manual also helped us refocus upon areas of our relationship that we consider important. Most critically, creating this Protocol Manual helped us craft (or return to) daily behaviors and rituals that communicate our love for one another.

I'd like to share a point-of-view with you: I think it will help you better understand this book.

In my experience, M/s structures differ somewhat from D/s structures. For example, there is less emphases on dominance and submission and more emphasis on leadership capability. In our case, Bob is far more outwardly dominant than I am, but he would be the first to tell you that he has neither vision nor leadership interest. He has "scholar" and "diplomat" archetypes; I have a "warrior" and "mama bear" archetypes. I ride the Harley while he follows in the car with about forty pounds of specialized camera gear and a tripod. I live on the edge; he lives in the world of collecting massive amounts of information on topics that interest him. He loves applying that knowledge in surprising ways. But, as I've said, he's an Aspie and those are pretty typical Aspie traits.

So: our relationship is that of two dominant people, one of whom has agreed to subjugate their will to the vision and guidance of the other.

Bob comes from the world of research. I get better compliance from him when he thoroughly understands the "why" of something. Because of this, I've included quite a bit of theory and background information. I've provided footnotes and some parenthetical comments to give readers background information that Bob would already know.

Since this book is, in fact, Bob's protocol manual, it's written as though I'm speaking directly to him. In this Manual, I use three voices, each of which carries a different meaning.

- <u>Very Important Issue</u>: I will speak like this to you. We are eyeball-to-eyeball.

- <u>The topic is a "directive</u>:" I will be telling the slave how it is to act. I am speaking; slave is objectified.

- <u>The topics are routine</u>: Master instructs the slave in this or that. I am referring to myself in "formal speech," so I am "Master."

Yes, much of the Manual's wording objectifies the slave; much is written in the third person.

This is how we live.

Section One
Putting this in Perspective

Our Contract

In exchange for providing emotional support and stability
and for providing relationship leadership,
you have agreed to subjugate your will to my vision
and to serve and obey thoughtfully and with an open heart.

My control over you is only circumscribed by one statement:
Master's wants must not trump slave's needs.

Archetypes exert an inexorable pull. They are like gravity in that way. Men and women are bombarded daily with subtle sociological nudges to act a certain way. Mostly, we're shown how to act as a boyfriend/girlfriend or husband/wife or father/mother. It's pervasive: we are exposed to this bombardment in movies, in romance novels, and in television ads. Against this backdrop, it can be challenging to keep a Master/slave dynamic alive and growing.

To avoid society's pull-to-normalcy (as you would phrase it)[1] one has to be aware that the pull is there and actively resist it. In our world, that means we must consciously do things to make our relationship special. If we didn't, mundane tasks will remain just that: mundane tasks.

However, we're not in a vanilla relationship; we're in a Master/slave relationship. In this setting, I, as Master, am in control of the psychological environment in which our relationship thrives or dies. I'm responsible for creating protocols leading to rituals that enable the mundane to have purpose.

I think some theory will help you understand my intent.

You elevate mundane tasks from *commonplace* to *interesting* by combining *intent* with *purpose*. When you intend something to be done a certain way for a particular purpose, you have a "protocol." In my world, you have a protocol for doing one kind of activity, such as "setting the table." *Setting the table* includes a number of sub-activities, but the overall protocol is only complete when the table is fully set, including centerpiece.

When you imbue a protocol with spiritual significance, it becomes a *ritual*. In the world of M/s, this is an important step. Without the spiritual aspect, the behavior would be no more than a habit. By the way, this is why rituals can get a bad reputation. Many people participating in a ritual are not involving their spirit; they are simply going through the motions. Because of this, a lot of people tend to overlook the value of ritual. You can elevate *ritual* to *magic* through theatrics.

Ceremonies result from combining a set of protocols into a spiritually-based practice. In our relationship, our "Evenings" (with the capital "E") are ceremonies.

It has been my experience that protocols/rituals/ceremonies help to hold M/s relationships together. In order to elevate our relationship above the level of "just partners," The protocols in your Manual are intended to cause our everyday life to be *unusual*. Taken as a whole, this Protocol Manual is intended to turn the mundane actions of living into a magical life that we celebrate nightly.

Your task, as my slave, is to piece this all together and make it work.

Conceptual Underpinnings

In my world, there is an important difference between Owner/property and Master/slave. The owner obtained their property as-is. The property accepted ownership as-is. The property had not signed up with their Owner to undergo any particular personal change. The Owner does not have the authority to request any fundamental change in the property.

That's not the case with Master/slave relationships as I understand and practice them. Here, the slave has specifically given authority over itself to its Master to do with as Master pleases. In this specific case, it pleases me that as my slave, you are always on your best behavior when serving me. I have written this Protocol Manual so you will always know what "best behavior" looks like to me.

Why change what you're doing?

Unless you change who and what you are, you'll always be who and what you now are. Many people are content with what they have already learned and how they act; others believe in lifelong learning. We are firmly in that latter group.

I believe that the more we are able to change the way we think and react to the world around, the more vital and interesting we become. I like interesting people. I want my slave to remain "interesting." I want my life to be "interesting." I expect you to help me expand both my knowledge and skill sets.

I once heard a saying that applies here; "Your dreams must exceed your capabilities in order to be pulled through life. After all, once you attain your dreams, what's left?"

Why protocols?

I wish to exert control over my immediate environment. I want help doing that. As my slave, that's your job. The success of your service resides in three words:

- Intent
- Focus
- Mindfulness

These three practices will lead you to competence and expertise in any area.[2]

Back to the question that heads this section: why protocols. In the same way that there are "normal accidents" in life, there are "normal problems" in relationships. I've found it much easier to resolve challenges that are anticipated than to resolve challenges that surprise you. In my world, proactive is better than reactive. As Master Obsidian says: "While the captain can control the ship, he can't control the weather." This Manual is about controlling the ship.

Master/slave structures focus on the interaction between two people: the person taking the "master" role and the person taking the "slave" role. The magic happens in the context of that interaction, and protocols drive that interaction.

- They keep us both "in the moment;"

- They focus my mind on how I wish things done in my world—perfectly, and with grace and elegance;

- They enable me to create a sacred vision of who we are and how we live.

Overriding requirements

My slave is required to be mentally awake and to interact with me using critical thinking skills. After that, your overriding requirements are:

- To obey my instructions;
- To anticipate and solve my problems; and
- To serve me with grace and elegance.

More specifically, you are to become exceptional in these skills and practices:

- <u>Formal personal services</u>: grooming, dressing, bathing, bedroom preparation, etc.;

- <u>Butlering services</u>: stocking household supplies, housekeeping in general, silver cleaning techniques, shopping, table setting for formal dining, etc.;

- <u>Gentlemanly skills</u>: erudite speech using 3rd and 4th definitions of words in addition knowing when to—and when not to—use high-level language;

- <u>Handyman skills</u>: know how to fix things, build things, repair things;

- <u>Sexual services</u>: be highly skilled at vaginal, anal, and oral, sexual stimulation;

- SM <u>play skills</u>: including but not limited to: impact play, e-Stim, fire play, insertion play, and vibrator play;

- <u>Evening-out services</u>: escorting me to social events, taking me out to dinner and/or dancing, taking me to nighttime entertainment;

- <u>Evening-in entertainment</u>: playing the piano, reading aloud, selecting computer-based entertainment to watch;

- <u>Visual pleasure:</u> physical appearance both clothed and naked; and

- <u>Sensual mood-setting services</u>: setting up fire in fireplace, candles, lighting, general ambiance.

All these will be covered in depth further in this manual.

Obedience

Obedience is different from *obeying*. It can come and go. Either Master's or slave's ego can block obedience. *Obedience* is **the** core value of our relationship. In this relationship, obedience is expressed through service as much as it is through action.

Living in obedience goes beyond doing only as you're told; it means the slave also wants only what the slave's Master wants.

When it comes to obedience, it is my responsibility to be sure you can succeed at an assigned task: it is your responsibility to complete the task fully and with an open heart.

To phrase this slightly differently, I'll make sure slave has the knowledge, skills, and tools to do what I am asking; the slave will do the job without internal grumbling.

The slave is responsible for keeping track of assignments. It is to alert me if I've assigned more tasks than it can manage, or a new task somehow interferes with a previously assigned task.

Those are nice, compact instructions. I'm to do X and the slave is to do Y.

No problem....

Except, the slave may have its own ideas about what it is to be a slave. It may even have private views about what it is to be MY slave. These contaminating thoughts create filters through which it hears me speaking.

I sometimes suspect the slave is obeying what it thinks I requested rather than what I *actually* requested. It seems to be obeying what it thinks is the best way to do the task, as opposed doing what I asked the way I requested.

When I first figured this out, I alerted my slave that it is to act in accordance with MY version of a slave and not its version of a slave. Actually, I pointed out that there was no "you" in this discussion: see Rule One (discussed in a few pages).

While there is still some friction over this, the process of writing this book has helped clear up important areas of misalliance.

Ego surrender

I agree with SlaveMaster (and some other highly regarded Leather Masters): slaves benefit psychologically by thinking of themselves as objects. Thinking of themselves as property helps them to stand aside from their own ego. This is referred to as *ego surrender*. Many who share this line of thought prefer their slaves to speak in the third-person—at least when discussing relationship issues with their Masters.

I, too, expect slave to be able to shift effortlessly between first-person and third-person speech.[3]

Attachment

My greatest fear is that the slave will develop *attachment,* not only to Master, but also to not having to make decisions. Please don't do that. As Yoda said: "Attachment leads to jealousy, the shadow of greed, that is. Train yourself to let go of everything you fear to lose."

Answering questions

In a general way, slave will be faced with two kinds of questions: questions of **fact** and questions of **opinion**.

I'll first address questions of *fact*, for there is a distinction you are to master.

When we're out in public (amongst Vanillas) slave may be forced to use **informal** speech when replying to a direct question. If so, your answers would sound like this:

- "Yes, that's right."

- "Yes, that's right, and you might wish to consider..."

- "That may be right, but I'm not sure. I think it may actually be..."

- "I'm afraid that I don't know. Would you like me to find out?"

I expect you to use these replies, as they enable you to give me a hint that I may have forgotten something or not quite known something. These phrases are noteworthy because none of them say "no" or oppose me in any way. These phrases honor our relationship.

In formal speech, it is my will that my slave responds to fact-based questions in this format: [4]

- "Yes, Master, you are correct, the answer is 'X'."

- "Yes, Master, you are correct and there is more that this slave knows related to this issue should Master wish to hear it."

- "No, Master, with respect, this slave believes the answer is 'Y'."

- "Master, this slave does not know the answer and will find out. To verify, this slave understands the question to be "Z." Does Master wish this slave to find the answer?"

I'll next address questions asking your *opinion* about something.

When I ask slave's opinion on a subject I expect just that: your opinion. slave is not being asked to make a decision; I will make the decision. slave is simply being asked for its opinion. Don't read more into it than that.

There will also be times when I make an observation that appears as a question. This is NOT a task assignment. Not everything I say requires action; an observation is simply that. When it becomes an assignment, there will be direction following the observation. I will not require slave to try to "decipher" what I've just said and what it may mean. For example, "Don't you think the garage is getting cluttered?" doesn't secretly mean: "Clean out the garage." It will only mean "clean out the garage" when I say, "Don't you think the garage is getting cluttered? Why don't you clean out the garage today? The slave is encouraged to ask questions to clarify its understanding of anything I say. The slave is also encouraged to respectfully point out anything relating to a task assignment that it suspects I may have overlooked. However, slave does not have the authority to refuse any direct request or order.

With regards to direct orders, slave has three response options:

- "Yes, Master: you are asking me to do 'X' and I will do that."

- "Yes, Master, if it pleases you that I do 'X,' I will do so."

- "Master, it will complete this task only if it pleases you, Master. Permission to restate my understanding of the task?"

There are two points, here.

First, slave will notice that it will restate its understanding of the task before starting the task. This will save the slave either from completing the wrong task or completing slave's (slightly incorrect) interpretation of what is being asked of it.[5]

Second, as slave is not permitted to say "no" to a direct order, the slave will use the "only if" construction to signal that it really would prefer not to do what I'm asking. Upon hearing the "only if" structure, I may or may not decide to probe further. Here are the rules governing my response to the "only if" phrasing:

- I will not force my slave through an "only if" response if I am angry with it.

- If I elect to require the slave to complete the task, it should know that in my heart I believe the slave will benefit from the lessons it will learn by working through its own barriers and upsets.

slave is also required to understand that my statements sel-dom require action. The statement, "I am hungry," does not mean that I wish something to eat; I'm simply remark-ing that I'm hungry. If I wished something to eat, I would state, "I would like something to eat." To my statement, "I am hungry," I expect no more reply than, "Yes, Master."

I am accustomed to saying exactly what I mean and what I want. slave is not responsible for reading between the lines to create meanings for my statements. slave is responsible only for understanding and acting upon sentences phrased as requests.

While I am generally a flexible person, there is one area for which I am inflexible. Refusal of a direct order expresses your personal will in opposition to my will. As our Contract re-quires you to follow my will with an open heart, an expression of willful disobedience represents your withdrawal from our relationship. This is not a topic open to further discussion.

Objectification

My slave is my property to treat as I deem appropriate. I will specify the slave's level of dress, grooming, and personal mannerisms. I will provide rules and instructions that govern the way my slave will interact with others. I will permit my slave to have controlled interactions with people I consider good and healthy and will prohibit my slave from interacting with those whom I consider harmful. As my slave has surrendered authority over its personal wishes to me, it's thoughts about such matters are of no consequence. I am committed to keeping my slave physically and emotionally safe. (Think *mamma bear and her cub.*)

I may permanently mark or modify my property as I wish.

Health and hygiene

The slave will maintain its physical appearance in a manner that pleases Master. As my slave is responsible for caring for my property, and as my slave is part of my property, the slave is responsible for caring for itself.

The slave's physical self: the slave will...

- Consume regular and nutritionally healthy meals.

- Obtain sufficient sleep to be able to attend to my needs.

- Keep its weight reasonably proportional to its height and build, specifically maintaining a flat belly and defined arm muscles. Pursuant to that, slave will exercise according to my specific instructions.

- Ensure that its fingernails and toenails are trimmed short. Manicures are encouraged, though not required. The slave will buff fingernails after clipping them.

- Trim its beard to $\frac{3}{8}$ths of an inch every Monday, Wednesday, and Friday. It will also shave its genital hair and underarms on those same days. The slave will attend daily to ear and nose hairs and keep its eyebrows trimmed. The slave understands that I expect this bullet point to be followed rigorously.

Medical expectations: the slave will...

- Maintain daily dental care that includes brushing its teeth, flossing its teeth, using a water pick, and any dental medical procedures suggested by its dentist.

- Have annual (or more frequent) examinations by the slave's medical providers (primary care physician, cardiologist, urologist, dermatologist, etc.).

  (Note: slave is encouraged to consider non-traditional healing paths, will propose and explain such treatments, and obtain permission before scheduling appointments.)

- Take such medications as are prescribed by its medical professionals.

- Be tested for STIs annually, at a minimum.

Rights and responsibilities

Concerning Master

I have all rights to the slave. There are no exceptions.

I am responsible for the following:

- Setting up and communicating the conditions that enable my slave to be successful in its service.[6]

- Finding areas that inspire my slave and supporting them within the context of our structure.

- Respecting previously negotiated limits.[7]

- Giving only ethical, lawful, and safe directives.

In a general sense, I am contractually responsible for slave's mental, physical, social, financial, and spiritual wellbeing. I am primarily responsible to act for the highest good of the Family; secondarily, I will act for the highest good of my slave.

I am responsible for the slave's continuing growth and development. In that light, I, as Master, must temper what is asked of the slave to ensure that the request is—at heart—congruent with the goals and intentions of our M/s relationship.

I recognize that as Master, "Choosing your battles" doesn't work. I must be consistent to establish reliability. This translates to a formal responsibility as Master: I am responsible for establishing and maintaining reliable and consistent behavior from my slave.

I recognize that any skill or service failure by the slave demonstrates my own failure as Master to provide effective training.

Concerning slave

My slave only has those rights specifically granted in this document.

Our M/s relationship is governed by three rules:

> Rule One: Master is right
> Rule Two: In cases of medical necessity, Master will follow the slave's guidance
> Rule Three: See Rule One[8]

I recognize that the slave's identity comes largely from serving me. I also realize that it is constantly looking for creative opportunities to serve. In this regard, I have a comment: I cannot overstress that the slave is responsible for providing my version (not its version) of service. As Raven Kaldera says: "If Master doesn't want it, it's not service." This protocol manual includes all the forms of service I seek from my slave. Please do not add others. If you think a new service should be added, discuss it with me: I'll decide whether it's useful.

Now: down to some specifics.

Master expects the slave to point out any potentially illegal or unethical aspect of an action being discussed. Similarly,

Master expects slave to mention any physical or emotional changes that might affect our play or the slave's service. In cases involving any kind of emergency, my slave is to act in the best interests of the relationship. Generally, that will be interpreted to mean: "Protect Master and yourself, in that order." Related to that, my slave is responsible for taking charge of the relationship if it is the slave's assessment that I am medically incapacitated or acting irrationally (due to medications or illness—see Rule Two).

My slave is responsible for controlling its emotional state. Since a person's reactions to events are under their control,[9] my authority governs the way you will react to me and to others.

As my slave, you do not have the authority to express personal upset over any of my orders or instructions. I understand that there may be times when you do, in fact, express upset and displeasure. When that occurs, slave is under its contractual obligation to speak transparently to me about the cause of its upset.

If you have become emotionally "triggered" by something I've said or done, you are to compose yourself and explain what's going on with you. I can't know how to address issues that you keep from me. I've noticed that your stoicism and drive to be my perfect slave sometimes conflicts with your transparency: I need to know how you think/feel about anything that pulls you from the path of focused, purposeful service.

If I sense that my slave is going to have trouble compos-
ing itself, we will use talking sticks to get to the root of
your upset. (See: Talking Stick Protocol in the section,
"Managing small upsets.")

The slave is responsible for remaining present, even when
upset.[10] The slave will not walk away from Master. It's not
polite under any circumstances, and in an M/s structure,
it dishonors the intent of the relationship. Remember, you
chose this Master. I did not choose you: I accepted you.

Here are a few more protocols that fall within your zone
of responsibility:

- If I'm concentrating on something, do not casually
  interrupt me. You must assess whether your need
  for my attention exceeds my need for private time.

- Under no circumstances will the slave leave my vi-
  cinity without permission. (slave may walk around
  the house or yard, but not leave the property.)

- If I'm *not* obviously concentrating on something,
  slave is free to approach.

- Once conversation has concluded, slave will bow,
  back up a bit, turn, and leave. The slave is not to
  turn its back on Master. Not polite.

The slave is responsible for helping Master make this relationship work. To that end, the slave is under an obligation
to point out why an action, order, or instruction may not
get the result the slave believes Master seeks.

The slave has the right to terminate and leave the relationship.

Time

I am sensitive to *time* and the way you use of it. I am *particularly* sensitive (and touchy) about having to wait for you. I'll discuss that in a minute.

"Time management" falls into a gray area for us. On the one hand, I want the products of your mind—as expressed in the books you write and the conversations we have. I also want the products of your networking skills, for you bring a rich assortment of interesting people into our lives.

On the other hand, in your role as my slave, you are not entitled to "free time" or "personal time," as such. Since slave's purpose is to serve Master, any *personal* action poses a direct conflict with the slave's reason for being a slave.

- If you need to do something during working hours that does not relate to our personal M/s dynamic, you are free to do that thing after texting me what you are going to do.

- If you plan to do something during working hours that *does* concern our relationship, you are obliged to obtain prior approval.

It is your responsibility to let me know *in advance* how much time you need for mental work (writing) or social networking. I'll let you know if writing/networking activities impinge on the time I need you to be available.

My specific instruction to you on this topic is that as slave, you are only entitled to your Master's preferences of beliefs. Thus, spending time on anything that falls outside my preferences and beliefs represents willfulness. You would be treading on very thin ice to spend time on something I don't know about. When in doubt, explain what time you need and how it supports our relationship.

Along this same line of logic, the slave may not waste my time. If I say we are leaving at "T" time, I expect my slave to be totally ready and waiting to leave before "T" time. You are advised not to cause me to wait for you. If slave suspects that it will be unable to keep a time commitment, slave must alert me immediately.

Here are a few more points to attend to:

- The slave has been given a certain amount of discretion concerning its professional work life. That means that if the slave's employer requires the slave to work during time that is usually under my control (such as working late at the office), the slave will follow its employer's demands but immediately inform Master of this situation. The slave will keep Master informed as the situation changes.

- The slave does not have the authority to make any commitments concerning my own time. Specifically, slave may not make any plans that involve me without prior discussion and approval. That includes social or business meetings as well as conference invitations.

To be clear: the slave is not to discuss "getting to-gether" with someone before obtaining my approval to approach them. You will explain the intent of the social or work event, and—if I agree to move forward—will check our calendars. After that, I will plan the approach to those involved.

When you act without my prior approval, you can count on my displeasure and unwillingness to participate. Your action has disrespected me and our relationship.

- Similarly, slave may not plan time with Master with-out Master's prior consent. Surprises are unwel-comed. Surprise parties are absolutely forbidden.

Being late without notifying me ahead of time is one of the very few areas that will make me angry.

Daily contact

I expect at all times to know where my slave is. My slave is my property; it is not a free agent. Since we are in touch by text during workdays, I expect my slave to notify me if it is going to be unavailable to reply to any text I might send. Similarly, I expect daily to be kept apprised of your general out-of-office schedule.

Here are some additional guidelines concerning times when you are traveling out-of-town without me.[11]

- Text me when you arrive at the airport, change planes, arrive at your destination, and arrive at your hotel. This is not controlling behavior: I need to know your travels have been safe.

- I'll text you when I can take your phone call: I expect to speak with you as soon as feasible, realizing that you are likely to be very busy once you reach your hotel. I also realize we are probably in different time zones. When we speak, you'll give me an outline of your evening plans and we'll schedule our evening Skype call.[12]

- If ANYTHING might cause you to be unavailable at the scheduled evening call-time, you will text me the revised time. I will automatically accept a revision within a 15-minute window before or after our scheduled call time. Beyond that, you are pledged to your word to contact me at our scheduled time. If there is a business reason preventing you from calling on Skype at that time, you will text a full description of the situation and I will tell you whether or not I will accept a different call time. Chances are, I will not, as I've arranged my schedule around our scheduled call.

- During our end-of-day Skype call, I expect a full and complete de-briefing including both social and business contacts.

How slave is to think of itself

The slave will align its reality with Master's reality. The slave has a history of creating its own reality and then reacting to that creation.[13] The slave is to learn strategies to become aware of such instances and to interrupt them. When in doubt about what is the correct and true reality, the slave will adopt Masters version of reality as its own. If the slave is having trouble adopting Master's reality, it will reflect on its contractual obligation to follow Rule One.

> A slave's reference to [itself] is understood to mean the part of [its] Master (or [its] Master's property) that consists of the slave's body, mind, and spirit. When a slave says (or writes) 'i,' it refers to the body and energies of the slave, but not [its] will, which as long as [it] is in service, is obedient to that of [its] Master. When a slave says 'my' or 'mine,' it means that part of the Master's property that is in the slave's keeping or stewardship—except, of course, in the phrases 'my Master or Mistress,' 'my slave brother or sister,' or 'my slavery' (the only thing that truly belongs to a slave).
>
> The Butchmann's Experience
> *Forms of Address*

Master's Expectations

I'm going to drop out of the formal M/s language I've been using up 'till now and speak directly to you as I describe my expectations. As you read, you'll understand why.

Compliance

Regardless of emotional closeness between us, I admonish you to remember always that you are subject to my will. In that light, you are required to comply with our Contract and with my orders and instructions.

I recognize that you have wrestled with releasing total control over your life and activities, particularly when we're not together. I'll remind you that you petitioned me: you asked me to guide you, repeatedly stating that you believed that I would produce a better future for you than you could do on your own. I accepted you under those terms.

I'll remind you, also, that under the terms of our Contract, you no longer have primary ownership over anything. Everything is owned either by me or *with* me. You are to refer to items as "ours." This includes friends, belongings, ideas, and activities. The only time you may refer to something as your own is if that "something" belonged to you in a past life or relationship (i.e., former wife, former Owner, former slave, children, college friends). If you continue to see friends from earlier times, they are now considered to be friends of the relationship and will be regarded as our friends.

Availability

Unless I know in advance, there is simply no time during the day or night when you may be unreachable. This includes times when you and I are out together, for instance, in different parts of the same store.

You are to keep me current with your daily activities, as already discussed, and I also want to know about after-work errands.

Correctness in public and private
Here's a good Butchmann's quote for you:

> A slave will always act and respond in such a way as to make the Master's orders look 'right.' A slave will never give the appearance that it thinks a Master has made a mistake, whether by facial expression, body language, or verbal challenge. Masters are not perfect, but whatever They order is 'right' because it is their will. It is the Master's will that the slave submits to, not its own sense of correctness. If the slave feels that [it] has information the Master is lacking, or sees a better possibility that [Master] has not considered, the slave may—within the limits of the protocol—ask whether Master wishes [it] to convey such information or to make a suggestion.

> The Butchmann's Experience
> *Obedience and Correctness*

During an evening with others, I require that you closely follow plans previously discussed/arranged. The rule is: "I don't like surprises and it's my game."

You represent me and this Leather Family by your appearance, words, and deeds whether we are together or apart. This holds true in all settings, whether kinky or vanilla.

You are to look, speak, and act appropriately at all times. Unless I specify a clothing style, you can wear what you wish.

We have a protocol that covers service hick-ups. Whether or not others are around, if you make some kind of service misstep, you are to continue without drawing attention to the lapse. If necessary, I will address the gaff privately, at a later time. I am certainly not going to point anything out in public. Not only do I not want to embarrass you, but any mistake you make reflects back on me for failing to adequately train you. If the situation is serious enough, I'll conduct an After Action Review in private.[14]

Obviously, rules of decorum are disregarded in actual emergencies.

Reliability and trust

The business world operates by identifying ways of being successful and then turning them into "defined repeatable processes." In other words, businesses replicate success through consistently doing things that work. In our M/s relationship, I expect you to perform tasks the same way each time. After all, what else are protocols?The actual process of following protocols has its own rewards. Successfully following protocols builds an environment of faithful obedience, respect, dedication, and trust.

There are two "value words" that relate to reliability and trust: those words are *honesty* and *dedication.*

Honesty. Two things about honesty: First, any "withholding" on your part means that you are controlling some aspect of yourself, thus opposing me. Second, unless you give me all relevant information on any topic, you're crippling my decision-making abilities. I will not have you limiting my decision-making abilities. You will be honest and forthcoming at the Contract level.[15] Deception plus guarded speech combine to create passive-aggressive behavior. If we have trouble at that level, we'll seek outside guidance. Such guidance may involve mediators, counselors, or therapists.

Dedication. By nature, ours is destined to be an intense relationship. It takes dedication and commitment to keep a high protocol 24/7 M/s relationship going. I am committed to building my leadership and communication skills and I expect you to develop commensurate skills.

Truth and openness

I understand that questioning you in some areas makes you uncomfortable. Sometimes, even asking your opinion makes you so uncomfortable that you essentially decline to answer. In my experience, when you dodge a question, you are really saying that you don't think I'll like your answer. Either there IS more going on than you will disclose, or you feel that a full answer would needlessly hurt my feelings. For the record, let me point out that you don't have the latitude to reach such an independent position. Under the terms of our Contract, you are ethically compelled to answer fully whether or not I like the answer. You have pledged to serve and obey me and there's no more to it than that. You are responsible for releasing your will to me.

You must answer.

And, although you know this, I will write it out here: *I will never punish you for telling the truth, although I may be disappointed in you as a person.*

In the spirit of our M/s relationship, I expect you to be pro-active in telling me if you've neglected to do an assignment, broken a rule, etc. You are required to answer my questions to the best of your abilities. You are further instructed to answer the intent of the question, not only the words of the question. You will take care not to omit any material information. Deception by omission or commission will be treated as lying. Lying is a violation of trust at the Contract level

I will not tolerate a partner that lies to me.

> slaves exist without privacy or defenses. What they are, whatever they do, and even what they think and feel must be open for inspection at all times. The slaves should always carry themselves with dignity, whether naked and in chains or out in the workaday world, and their appearance and behavior should always reflect positively on their Master and their slave brothers and sisters.
>
> The Butchmann's Experience
> *Openness*

This discussion of "openness" crosses over to the world of emails and new relationships.

I expect to be informed when you would like to initiate contact with someone new who might become more than a casual friend. I expect to be involved at the point that you think sex play is a likely outcome. After we discuss the situation, I either will or will not give you permission to proceed. I may wish to be copied on correspondence until I am comfortable that you're not putting yourself at emotional or psychological risk with this person. As a matter of practice, this requirement is withdrawn once I have a sense of the honor and integrity of the relationship. Once I inform you to stop copying me on your messages, I then only wish to be kept generally apprised of the relationship.

I'm not going to like it if I learn that a flirtation has developed without my knowledge.

The *disappointment* loop

I am sometimes disappointed in you. Perhaps I've set my expectations too high; perhaps you're just a bit "off" that day. In any case, I want to bring this to your attention so you can work on it.

To set the stage, let me be clear that I am capable of taking care of my own needs. Furthermore, I am capable of taking care of my own needs while also taking care of your needs. You should know, though, that once expressed, I am accustomed to having those needs attended to. If I tell you what I want or need and you don't attend to it promptly,

I am likely to take care of it myself. Sometimes I'll choose to be upset with your lapse of attention; sometimes I won't. My response will depend upon my understanding of your capabilities and intentions.[16]

I realize and understand that when I attend to my own needs or wants, my actions are running counter to our structure. Over our years together, I've found it's sometimes simply easier to leave you out of the loop. You mean well, but I'm not willing to wait for you to notice your laps. Your loop of inattention looks like this:

- I've told you (or shown you) what I need;

- Either you didn't notice or didn't hear my need (through your own inattention or distraction);

- Instead of asking again, I do it myself.

You are always very apologetic and rush to try to make things better, but the fact is, you missed the mark. I've prepared this Protocol Manual after a great deal of consideration. It's intended to help to stabilize the target for you. As you are serving me, I owe it to you to explain precisely the level and extent of service I require. My goal, here, is to strengthen our relationship in order to attain seamless communications and interactions. I'll know we've attained this goal when your service anticipates my needs and becomes effortless action. This is termed *invisible anticipatory service* and it is rare, indeed. Since this is our path, I decided we needed to record the steps we've taken to get there. Hence, this Protocol Manual. This is your personal book of "defined, repeatable processes."

Managing small upsets

Upsets occur for many reasons, of course. Frequently, they occur when there is a mismatch of background knowledge between people and one person's knowl-edge-and-experience-based assumptions of *the right thing to do* crashes into another person's equally solid knowledge and experience-based assumptions. To move beyond upset, we have to work diligently to identify gaps in knowledge or experience.

In our case, we have some important differences between us. For starters, you are 20 years older than I am. Beyond that, we were brought up very differently, we were educated very differently, and we have substantially different factual knowledge bases. I've crafted a series of protocols to help us through these differences.

As you've experienced, I'm very quick to sense a "distur-bance in the force," as it were. If I can get you to come present that something is going wrong and then get you to speak from your adult ego-state, I can generally lead you through whatever has disturbed you. (Note: "Adult ego state" is a term from Transactional Analysis. The other two "emotional ego states" are *parent* and *child*.)

I prefer to stop your upsets before they turn into an Asperger spiral and affect your behavior. I've found two questions sometimes help:

- "What did you hear me say that triggered you?"
- "What did you make that mean?"

Sometimes this approach works, sometimes you become evasive. If I am able to pull you out of your reactive state, I'll ask: "What do I need to say to right now to bring you peace?" I'll admit, though, I've never been able to get this far. You either regain your self-control or I have to go to Plan B. I usually have to go to Plan B.

Plan B is our "Talking Stick" protocol. This is the only way I've found to produce cerebral (rather than emotional) responses from you. I need your "adult ego voice" in order to understand the root of the upset.

Talking Stick Protocol

- I will ask you to get (or you will bring to me) our talking stick and bring it to the living room. We will sit on the couch next to one another.

- I will place the talking stick between us.

- One of us will pick up the stick and explain their understanding of the upset. They may speak uninterrupted until done.

- The speaker puts the talking stick down.

- To be sure that the communication is clear, the person who was listening must repeat what the other person said.

- The talking stick is put down.

- This goes on until both of us agree on the nature of the upset. Once that is agreed upon, the other person may respond.

- The responding person picks up the stick and offers their response.

- To be sure that the communication is clear, the person listening must repeat what the other person said.

- The speaker puts the talking stick down.

By this point, we have only our respective interpretation of the event that caused the upset. We now will continue to use this process until the issue is fully understood and resolved.

If we both go out of control and can't use the Talking Stick Protocol, I've found it best to remove myself from your presence. You generally use this time to write about what happened.

You like to write. You are able to think more clearly after you have "vented" in your journal. While I prefer that you vent directly to me, I've found this is not your way. You realize that when you are upset you risk saying things that you can't take back. So: when I sense that you need time get poisonous ideas out of your head I will say something to the effect of: "This conversation is over. You may want to write in your journal."

You are to follow this two-step process when venting in your Journal:

- Your first description of your upset should be filled with emotional words. I would prefer that you do this in longhand where you can't delete any words, but I realize that you type faster than you write, and your handwriting is hard to read.

- Next, go to your computer and rewrite the upset as facts only. Try to think of yourself as a video recorder. Report your actions/statements and then mine.

If you are able, I'd then like you to come to me so we can discuss how our worldviews had collided and how we can avoid it in the future.

When I judge that you are again in a calm, adult frame of mind, I will ask: "Are you ready to resume your role as slave?"

Managing large upsets

I distinguish between two kinds of large upsets and I'll approach them separately.

- An event that immediately threatens a core value of our relationship, and

- A festering dissatisfaction.

Relationship shaking event

We will use the "Red Eight-Ball Protocol."[17]

If either of us refers to our red eight-ball when others are around, we will immediately excuse ourselves from that setting and discuss the situation. Clearly, one of us has missed something that's going on. There is no exception to this protocol, even if one of us is laughing or seemingly joking when saying, "red eight-ball."

If we are alone, if one of us needs to have a relationship-level discussion, they will place the red eight-ball and the talking stick together in a conspicuous place. Within a reasonable period (say, 15 minutes), the other person is to compose themselves and join the other person sitting by the red eight-ball. From there, we use our talking stick protocol.

You are having "issues" about our relationship
I recognize that you have Asperger Syndrome and your reality can sometimes differ from my reality. I also recognize that you generally benefit from being left alone to work through your issues. Although I don't much like you telling others about our upsets, I have found it prudent to permit you to speak about your upset with:

- A Leather brother or sister;

- A person whom we have previously used as a mediator or mentor; or

- A professional counselor/therapist.

Now: by allowing you to work with those three categories of helpers, I am NOT allowing you to discuss your upset(s) with anyone else until I am fully informed and have had a chance to consider and respond. You are specifically prohibited from discussing anything about our relationship with friends or former partners.

Since this topic is a touchy one between us, I'm going to expand on this protocol.

- Yes, you can work with those three categories of helpers to flatten your upset.

- No, you may not use those people to "build a position" on some topic that concerns our relationship.

I understand that displays of willfulness of the kinds I'm discussing represent an outcry of distress in our relationship. For you to be willful means we have a deep relationship issue. If you can't resolve whatever is bothering you within a day or so, we're likely to need to call one of our mediators. Thus, you are charged with keeping me informed of your progress resolving whatever is eating at you.

I expcot you to speak with me when you have a growing or (apparently) unresolvable concern either about our relationship or about me. Failure to inform me is an "error of omission" tantamount to lying. We have already covered this point.

This is the end of the part where I spoke directly to you. I'll now go back to my usual M/s-language.

Specific Issues

slave's mastery

In this relationship, Master expects the slave to master the art of service and obedience. As previously mentioned, expertise is accomplished through intent, focus, and mindfulness.

My slave is expected to continue to grow emotionally and academically in order to broaden slave's outlook on life and learn new skills. The slave is expected to continue to read broadly and to take such classes, workshops, or courses as needed to support its continued research and writing.

The slave is expected to apply this knowledge for the relationship's benefit.

Master recognizes and supports the slave's passion for learning and the slave's (eccentric-seeming) attitude that every moment it's not in service, eating, sleeping, or working it must be pouring knowledge into its head.[18]

Viewpoint

In this relationship, *protocols* define the way the slave will serve its Master. They also define the way Master wishes to be treated. In fact, protocols enable the slave to demonstrate perfect service and obedience on a daily basis.

Protocols are a vehicle to help the slave remain focused and purposeful. They are a way for slave to "come present" with its service. Mastering protocols is something like mastering a dance form; it takes daily practice and focused concentration until the movements and processes become second nature.

Grace, elegance and lucidity

Master seeks to build an environment that exudes grace and elegance.

- The slave is responsible for identifying and employing ways of incorporating graceful movement into its presentation and style. For example, the slave will remain aware of the sound of it's footfalls and work to remove sound from it's movements.

- The slave is responsible for being sensitive to its dress and appearance at all times. In our Family, slave is expected to be *slightly overdressed* on all public occasions.

Effortless technique as a concept

"Effortless technique" is the key concept underlying all its actions. In this Household, everything is to look effortless. For example, all food preparation for a meal is to be complete at the same time. If the slave is serving a plated meal (that is, all the food is placed on the plate while it is still in the kitchen) slave is also responsible for artfully presenting the food. The slave is responsible for keeping a supply of such things as candied apples, spiced peaches, fresh parsley, apples, oranges (and the like) on hand for this purpose.

True mastery is often expressed by the apparent ease with which the practitioner carries out a function or task. Master expects the slave to be so competent at tasks that others observing will not see or be distracted by the **work** or **effort** involved. This includes our protocols, but even extends beyond them into every aspect of its service.

Family structure
Rules governing family relations
This Family can be viewed as a "team" in the business sense of the word. Many of the rules and guidelines for building strong teams apply equally for building a strong Family. In summary, they are:

- Be loyal to those not present: Family members will not discuss Family issues with others. No personal information about Family members will be shared with others. Parenthetically, if slave hears someone speaking ill of another family member, slave will suggest that they find a way to discuss it directly and constructively with the person.

- Don't complain to others: If slave has a concern or complaint, slave will bring it to Master. Concerns and complaints will receive a better reception if they are presented as an area to work on instead of an accusation of neglect in an area.

- Do more than your fair share: I recognize that much is required of my slave. But that's the nature of the deal. While I'm working very hard to create a Magical World filled with intellectual and emotional stimulation, I need slave to be searching relentlessly for ways of helping proactively.

- Be dependable: Be where I expect slave to be, when I expect slave to be there, and prepared to do the job-at-hand. If something is to happen at a certain time, slave will be ready before that time—even if Master is not ready. Master will not wait for slave and will proceed with the event/activity without slave.

- <u>Anticipate what I am going to do next</u>: Good Family members rarely need to tell one another what to do next because the partner is already doing it.

- <u>Be flexible</u>: The slave must be prepared to follow quickly, and without fully understanding the why behind the requested action. The slave must learn to recognize when I am in "problem-solving" mode and learn to interject refining questions at that time—not *after* we've made a decision.

slave's obligations
In rank order, the slave's obligations are to its:

- Master
- Biological family[19]
- Leather Family
- Local Leather Community
- Leather Tribe

Communication
Speaking/Gesturing
When speaking, the slave will modulate its voice to be as pleasant as possible—never loud, or strident. The slave will speak slowly and enunciate clearly.

The slave will always be aware of the effect of words on others (direct meaning as well as connotation) and be keenly aware of when to change the subject or when to stop speaking altogether.

Many times there will be non-verbal clues from listeners reflecting their conversational comfort level. While slave should be sensitive to these cues, slave is not to shoulder this responsibility without Master's help—due to slave's Asperger condition.

Timely and relevant

Master is to know immediately if something comes up in the slave's life that concerns our relationship in general or Master, in particular. Master wants such information immediately, not at home after work. Should Master be unavailable by phone until lunch breaks or work is closed, slave is to send a text requesting a phone call. The slave is to clearly indicate urgency.

The slave's role is to remove problems from my life, not to add problems. Small issues can grow larger if not caught early. Timely communication about important issues is basic to our structure.

Communication with others

Under normal circumstances, the slave is free to email any-one it wishes. The slave is aware that its email will always be available for Master's review.

Here is my guidance about communicating with others about us:

- slave will present Master (and slave's relationship with Master) in a positive light.

- slave will not discuss Master beyond explaining that, "Master is doing well, thanks for asking." Unless covered by Rule Two, the slave is specifically prohibited in providing any personal details about Master to *anyone* without first obtaining very specific permission to do so.

- slave will not discuss its relationship with Master other than to say the slave is well and happy—even if the slave has previously shared more openly with that person.

The slave has one Asperger trait that is relevant to this "communications with others" topic. Sometimes, the slave does not fully grasp that its precise written communication may sometimes be misinterpreted. While those you know well understand your meaning, the same cannot always be said of others. Because of this, it is our protocol that the slave will send to Master for review, all draft correspondence that in any way refers to or involves Master.

As a courtesy, I would like you to copy me on all eMail to ANY Dom/Domme or Leatherman so I can keep current with the slave's plans and ideas. This does NOT mean that I want to be copied on all its emails, just those that contain information I'll need to keep up within the kink life that we share. Limits on the slave's communication freedom were covered earlier under: "Truth and openness" and "Handling relationship upsets."

No arguments

Arguments involve drama. They represent the pitting of one person's will against another's. Since Rule One states that Master is right. There is never a reason to argue. The slave is encouraged to ask for clarification if it does not understand something. The slave is also encouraged to share issues that trouble it (or bring it joy).

The slave will assiduously avoid asking "leading questions" or using argumentative expressions of opinion. The slave is always to consider itself to be Master's property, wholly focused on fulfilling Master's will.

At Master's discretion, Master and slave may discuss any matter at all. However, they do not argue!

Correction[20]

I distinguish between punishment and correction. I can understand the need to punish the slave for an ethical breach, but punishing someone who is voluntarily serving has never made sense to me. This is particularly true if the offense concerns a protocol violation. It's better to laugh it off and then figure out how the lapse happened.

Correction (as it relates to protocol violations) will include Master expressing disappointment, minor *funishments* (swats), and more serious warnings against future reoc-currences of the unwanted behavior. If the slave continues to have trouble executing a particular protocol, we'll discuss what is going wrong and how to modify the protocol to avoid repeated glitches.

I'm cautious about the entire concept of "punishment" within consensual authority-imbalanced structures. I'm leery because the slave has volunteered to serve, and (as a general rule) works extremely hard at it. In my Household, correction and punishment are used very sparingly, lest the slave becomes overcritical of their own actions and wary of Master's scrutiny. *I am also particularly careful to distinguish between correcting slave's behavior versus correcting slave as a person.* I want to love and cherish the person while correcting behavior.

I am reminded of a saying I heard some years ago: "Managing a slave perfectly is like playing an instrument perfectly; beating a violin won't make it play better."

Punishment and atonement

I do not love punishment. Punishment may contain pain, but it also contains disappointment. It contains the element of displeasure that breaks my heart.

As I've repeatedly said, "punishment" is reserved for an egregious breach of trust at the Contract level. A breach at this level reveals a character flaw. Relationships dissolve over character flaws. Examples include: overt dishonesty, acting purposefully against me or the known best-interests of the relationship, or by purposefully harming another in a way that brings shame on our union.

While one expects that a relationship will make it from beginning to end without such a crushing breach of trust, it is prudent to plan for the possibility. Rather than get caught unaware, I'm going to outline my likely approach. (I ascribe to the sentiment: "Plan like a pessimist, live like an optimist.")

Here are some ground rules:

- I'm not going to discuss this with the slave when I'm hurt and angry.

- Before I decide how to react, the slave will have the opportunity to fully explain how this situation developed and where, in retrospect, it should have behaved differently. The slave will also explain to my satisfaction HOW it should have behaved and the logic that caused it *not* to behave that way.

- After hearing the slave's version of reality, I'll think about what it said. I'm likely to send it out of my presence at this point. I may send it to spend a few nights elsewhere.

- If I choose not to release my slave on the spot, I will begin by asking it whether it is *willing* to discuss and resolve the meaning of this outrageous willful behavior.[21]

If "yes," the discussion continues.

If "no," I will take it that you have withdrawn from the relationship. Relationship termination protocols are covered immediately after this topic.

Presuming that the relationship is to continue, punishment will be immediate. The infraction and reason for the punishment will be discussed. Once the punishment has been completed, it is over. It will not be brought up again. The slave is expected to learn from its mistakes.

If the cause triggering the need for punishment is truly serious, I'll approach the entire topic more carefully. Depending on how the discussion develops, I may ask the slave to recommend a course of action to address the root causes of whatever it is that caused it to defile the relationship. On the other hand, I may ask the slave to propose a process of punishment and atonement to encapsulate the experience and remove it from the relationship. The consequences—and the way I'll approach my slave—are completely situational.

I will listen to the slave's proposal(s), consider them, and then announce the correct course.

In a general sense,

- I will use the minimum influence necessary to compel the slave's compliance with the policies and procedures slave has previously agreed to.

- I will not punish slave with play. Punishments will never be fun.

- If I wish the relationship to continue, there are no limits to the nature or extent of punishment that could be ordered as a result of the slave's act of willfulness or negligence so long as no crime is committed (battery, death). In reality, in our relationship, *punishment* takes the path of restrictive Instructions about the use of slave's time and/or withdrawal of the slave's time with me.

- After administering the prescribed punishment, the slave and I will sit down and discuss relationship changes meant to ensure that no such breach can occur again. This may mean that the slave is now on probation and risks dismissal.

- I will observe how the slave manages during its re-covery from its recklessness and thoughtlessness. Once I feel the slave is again stable, I will design ac-tions for the slave to atone for the damage it's done to our relationship. Once I'm satisfied that the slave has fulfilled my requirements, the subject will not be brought up again by either of us. Atonements are for the injured party, not for the party who did the damage. The atonement process may take years. Once broken, trust is very slow to heal.

Terminating the relationship

Relationships tend to end in one of two ways: they die for lack of interest or they explode over violation of trust.

Termination through apathy

We'll work it out. Since there will only be a kind of sadness for what could have been, there is no drama or urgency to close down the house and go our separate ways.

Termination through egregious ethical breach

If your actions trigger a relationship crisis and tell me that you are not willing to work through it, you are now released from my service.

You will follow this dissolution procedure to the letter.

- I will decide which one of us will leave.

- All further communications will be through email. You will not phone or text me.

- Some amount of time will pass. It could be hours or days.

- At my choosing, I'll inform you of the dates that one of us has to pack and move possessions.

- If many weeks separate the period between your release from service and one of us moving out, I will inform you either when you are to be out of the house or when I will arrange to be out of the house. We will not again be together in what was once our shared home.

- Whichever of us leaves will be responsible for paying their portion of our monthly expenses for one month following departure.

- You will not attend any local kink functions for 30 days and we will coordinate not to attend the same functions the following 30 days. This is a cooling off period necessary to separate emotions following a hurt.

Section One Footnotes
Footnotes 1-21

1   You're going to have to get used to these footnotes. There are a lot of them. However, many of them are really interesting, such as this one.

Bob is a "wordsmith." We literally have over 100 books on words, word origins, symbols and such. We also have the multi-volume print edition of the Oxford English Dictionary—a collection of books each weighing fifteen pounds that consume 40" of shelf-space. Yes, I just counted the books: yes, I just measured the OED.

I'm giving this background because without it, you'd miss some of the playfulness with words that he's stuck into this book. "Normalcy" is one of the words you'd likely miss. I have learned from him that this is an example of an "inkhorn" word. A word made by someone (figuratively) dipping their quill pen into an inkhorn and writing it down. Many words enter our language this way, LOL. In this case, "nomalcy" is a word used by President Warren Harding to describe the calm political and social order to which he wished to return the United States after the idealism and commotion of the presidency of Woodrow Wilson. However, the word didn't exist until he used it in his speech. Presumably, he'd meant "normality."

2   Every one of these three practices takes work, of course. And in our entertainment-driven culture, "work" is usually relegated to something you're paid for. As a result, people generally have rather hazy goals about what they're going to be doing for the next week, month, or five years. The problem with that is that hazy goals produce hazy results. So: to avoid hazy results, you might consider clearly defining your goals. Unfortunately, if you have a problem defining your goals, you have a problem.

3   For those unfamiliar with third-person speech in daily communication, it goes like this: "Does Master require anything of this slave for the next fifteen minutes, or is it released to begin preparing dinner?"

4   When we become even slightly stressed in our rela-tionship, we revert to formal speech protocols. This immediately changes our emotional state and makes conversations much more precise. In the language of Transactional Analysis, this forces both of us to speak from our "adult ego-state." The two other ego states are parent and child. The parent ego-state is filled with anger, judgment, and scolding; the child ego-state is filled with crying, emotional words, and tantrums.

5   In communication theory, this is called "active listen-ing." The listener repeats the key elements of what the speaker said and waits for the speaker either to agree that's what they said, or restate what they said to be more precise. The listener then restates

the revised version to be sure that he/she NOW understands the statement or request.

6   Master is responsible for ensuring that slave serves Masters version of mastery, not its version of what it wants as a master.

7   If we have discussed pushing or expanding slaves limits, Master may do so, but Master will not breach what slave has communicated as hard limits.

8   The phrase, "see Rule One" means that whatever the slave may think about something is of no consequence in the face of Master's views or opinion about that "something." Master is always right, as stated in Rule One.

9   See Footnote 4. Also, people have (or can learn to have) control over how they express their emotional states. Think about professional actors. When you see them in movies and on TV, they're not sad when they're crying and they're not happy when they're laughing: they've learned to portray those emotions through what is called "state control" by those familiar with Neuro Linguistic Programming (NLP).

10   "Remaining present" can be difficult to explain. Let me do it this way. When something is done, it's over. Once it's over, you go on to the next thing. There is an intersection between "over" and "next." That's where you live when you are "living in the moment," and that's where you are to go when you are interacting with me, particularly during an upset.

11   We lecture and make presentations all over the coun-
      try and throughout Canada. Sometimes Master can-
      not travel either for financial reasons or because I
      cannot get leave time from work.

12   We've found that seeing one another when speaking
      (as opposed simply to using our cell phones) makes
      a tremendous difference to both of us. It keeps our re-
      lationship bond tight even though we are not together.

13   The situation wherein someone creates their own
      "story" of something said and then reacts emotionally
      to that story is called "projection." This psychological
      theory was first described by Carl Jung in 1938. This
      topic is well known; it's easy to find good information
      about it. The key concept is that people interpret re-
      ality based on their own personal experiences and
      belief systems and often ascribe their own beliefs
      or behaviors to others and then have an emotional
      reaction along the lines – 'Had I said that I would
      have meant this so they must mean this'. This can be
      baffling to the other person, for you're blaming them
      for behaviors that never occurred to them. That is, the
      objective reality of what happened is different from
      the subjective story you've made up about what hap-
      pened. When you react to your version of the story,
      the other person is baffled at what they see as your
      distortion of the facts.

14   "After Action Reviews" come from the Military. We
      discuss three things that went well and three things
      that could have gone better.

15   "...at the Contract level" means that violating "X" is breaking the fundamental commitment to serve and obey Master in exchange for... Violations at "the Contract level" are grounds for dismissal.

16   "Choose to be upset." Section of personal mastery involves mastering your emotional self. The problem with "being upset" is that those very words communicate that your state-of-being is upset. This suggests that you are not in control. Your "lizard brain" has control of you.

With practice, you can learn to identify situations that previous triggered you. You can interrupt your old pattern of behavior and chose your reaction. You may choose to call a "time out;" you may choose to be uncharacteristically calm and quiet; you may choose to have a melodramatic overreaction. The issue, though, is that YOU are in charge of your reaction to the situation. You are Master of yourself.

17   When we were developing this protocol, we felt we needed some truly unusual phrase that would communicate the emergency to the other person, particularly if others were around. Well: Bob has a 5"x12"x 5" art-piece of twelve black 8-balls (representing a jury) with a lid that closes to make the box appear to be a small coffin (the trial wasn't going well for the defendant). We thought we would use the 8-ball symbolism to signify "trouble." Of course, 8-balls are black: a cold color. We wanted a color to represent the upset emotional state that we'd be in when

evoking it. Red. Red 8-ball. We bought a red 3-ball (not a problem) and had an artist friend convert the 3 to an 8. It sits on our fireplace mantle in a little plastic stabilizing disk.

18   The slave makes it a practice to read the news on his cell phone when going to the toilet.

19   Biological family... this slave is 71 at this time. Its parents are dead and children are in their mid-30s. The slave wanted this list to reflect its personal feelings about the order of its obligations.

20   Punishment is not an appropriate response to a protocol violation: if the slave is having trouble executing a protocol, either the protocol is too complicated or the protocol somehow exceeds the slave's mental or physical powers. Since it is Master's responsibility to train the slave to use Master's preferred protocols, protocol failure represents training failure.

21   The word "willing" carries a special meaning for those who have gone through The Butchmann's Experience. Master can only lead to the extent that the slave is willing to follow and serve. Often, when Master asks this slave to do something, Master ends the request/order with the question: "Is the slave willing to do this?"

Section Two
Basic Service

Protocols that enable one to live as we do are not acciden-tal. As previously mentioned, the protocols developed by an M/s couple are outgrowths of their values. In our case, the fact that my father was career Military and that my slave is an Aspie who needs routine and orderliness conspire to create our preference for living as we do.

I've asked my slave why he keeps the house in a showroom state. He gives two answers. First, he says, it's a form of meditation, a way of practicing mindfulness. Second, he says, he uses "immaculate house" and dressing well as love messages. I get it. I can see his love in how it keeps the house, why he serves elegant dinners, and how he dresses and speaks as he does.

I certainly enjoy the fruits of his work, but it's a gawd-awful amount of work.

Over the last year, we've documented the steps we take to establish and maintain this state. Actually, this chapter describes the process of *doing things the right way*. It's a blueprint, should you wish to follow this path.

Protocol Review

These policies and procedures will be reviewed and revised periodically, as Master directs. Master will consider the slave's occasional request for a protocol review.

Suggestions by the slave to changes any part of this document must be in writing and include these four headings:

- Current wording
- Proposed wording
- Reason for request.
- Practical advantage in making this change?

Interacting with others
Interacting with guests to our home
With rare exceptions, guests to our home are already know to us from our BDSM and M/s communities. As such, hugs are assumed unless the event is a High Protocol Leather evening. The combinations of options are too great to set out here. In a general sense, I expect my slave to act more like a butler: remain aloof but available.[22]

We have found only two areas to be challenging with guests: BDSM play and sexual contact. Because my slave has a (well deserved) reputation for sexual techniques with women,[23] he is approached fairly frequently by women who want that experience. Because of this, I want to know in advance what the guest(s) and what my slave might be considering. I require pre-negotiation for play, whether or not it involves intercourse. There are no exceptions to this. If I have not been in direct negotiation with all the involved parties, then guests will be coming to share a meal with us and no more.

I'm not opposed to permitting sexual touching and play with my slave, but I want to know specific expectations before the get-together. While I may be willing to co-Top, it is extremely unlikely that I will be involved in any other role. Under zero conditions will I bottom.

Interacting at not-Leather events

At munches, parties, workshops, etc. the slave is generally free to offer/receive/return hugs. If the person wishing to be hugged is not well known to us, my slave will look to me for approval. If the person seeking a hug is another slave, my slave will accept the hug after obtaining my permission. We assume the other slave's Owner/Dominant gave them permission to hug my slave.

Other than hugs, no one is to touch my slave in any way without my explicit permission. Similarly, unless it is to aid in an emergency, my slave is not to touch anyone without permission both from me and, if another slave, from their Owner. "Flirty touching" that is non-sexual is permitted so long as it's just that.

Interacting at Leather events

By "Leather setting" I mean a local, regional, or national event intended for Leatherfolk. This could be an informal Leather club meeting, a Leather bar, or a Leather conference.[24]

I expect Leatherfolk at Leather events to understand when we are in protocol and will respect my slave's position within our Family.

Now: some special situations can arise at weekend Leather/BDSM events that are unique to my own slave. Master recognizes that the slave's background as an author and presenter on M/s and other topics means that it is fairly well known. In many cases, my slave has known these people for over a decade. Also, we are usually vending at conferences. In these situations, the slave will introduce Master to friends as quickly as possible and will endeavor to brief Master regarding any relevant background about the person.

When at formal social events within the conference, the slave will remain in default position (to Master's right) when feasible. The slave is released from this protocol when conversing with speaking with an established friend, in which case the slave will include Master in the conversation.

In my experience, my slave's position in the Leather community appears to be the same as a senior uncapped Master. When interacting with other presenters and attendees, my slave is to follow protocols that govern interaction at that rank.[25]

Titles
My slave represents me. When speaking with others, my slave is expected to be polite and respectful at all times and will call/address others by their known title as a sign of respect and politeness.

At BDSM events, the slave will refer to a person using the name that seems most appropriate. When someone introduces themself using both their scene name and their given name, the slave will use their legally given name. If the person is using the "Master" title with little or no known experience, the slave may speak with them in such a way that their name does not come up. This avoids the issue of having to refer to them as "Master Bigdog" or some such. In the presence of Leatherfolk, Masters shall be afforded their due respect and slave will refer to them by the honorific by which they are introduced. During conversations, covered Masters will be referred to as "Master..." When ending the conversation, my slave is to say something to the effect: "It was really good seeing you Master "X," I hope you enjoy the rest of the conference."

NOTE: It is NOT appropriate for slave to converse casually with another slave while in active service to Master. If Master and slave are watching a play scene (or even vending), the slave is considered to be 100% in service and the slave must first obtain my permission to carry on a social conversation.

Should a Leatherslave endeavor to hug my slave without having first negotiated with me, my slave will graciously return the hug. My slave will be careful to avoid publicly embarrassing this person by explaining that it is in service. My slave may mention that this approaching slave is welcome to speak with its Master (me) to obtain permission for physical contact in the future. If this situation reoccurs, the slave will inform the novice Leatherslave that it is in High Protocol and—with respect—does not have permission to return the second hug. The slave will promptly report the incident.

Interacting with me
Our public presentation
I have come to view our interaction in this unusual M/s relationship as a celebration of our union and the fact that we are alive, well, and economically comfortable. I wish this to be apparent to those who see us together. In that light, it is my will that we are mindful of our dress, speech, and behavior when in public. This includes the way we eat hot dogs at the beach, fried rice at an Asian restaurant, or walking down the street. I wish to present us in a particular way in public. I wish us always to be a little bit dressed up, and I wish us to be slightly formal in public. I realize I'm rather "preaching to the choir" to say this to my particular slave, as it wears a suit every day, but I want to include it in the protocol manual to be sure we don't lose track of it.

As Master is not comfortable socializing in large groups (and can, in fact, become claustrophobic), the slave is to remain within Master's line of sight, preferably close enough that Master can speak with it when Master wishes. The slave is not to leave Master's side without explicit permission. Should we find ourselves separated by conversations within the same room, slave will remain within Master's line of sight and will always monitor Master's body language. If Master appears uncomfortable, the slave will stop its conversation and return to Master's side.

If we're speaking together and someone approaches and appears to want to engage in conversation with slave, the slave is somehow to communicate to this person that it is not the person in charge and that their question / opening line must be directed to me.

Speaking

My slave is encouraged to speak to me at all times, remembering that after work I require a certain amount of decompression time. Master will inform slave when Master is ready for normal interaction.

The slave has no speech restrictions whatsoever when vending at conferences. While I can't cover all situations, here are some common settings and my preferences for my slave's level of speech. These protocols are in effect at all times, as the slave is always in service to me, whether or not we are together.

- If attending vanilla events, the slave is to be reserved.

- In non-vanilla settings, the slave will make certain that others understand our M/s dynamic.[26]

- At Leather events, the specific situation dictates the level of speech restriction. Thus, if it is a cigar social, the slave is free to socialize while using standard social protocols. However, if we are attending any of the formal ceremonies (including the Leather Social), slave will be in High Protocol and under low speech restrictions.[27]

- At any event where we are participating in anything carrying a "High Protocol" designation, the slave will be under total speech restriction.

- In a general sense, my slave will only initiate conversation with a collared submissive or slave after first obtaining permission from me. If I grant permission, either my slave or I (depending on the specific situation) will then approach the slave's Master/Owner and ask permission to speak with their property.

Speech and stance protocols communicate the formality of our M/s dynamic. We will use such protocols as a way to share "who we are" as a couple. These protocols serve as a way to help us maintain our relationship focus.

Using furniture

In our home, the slave is permitted to use furniture unless otherwise directed.

I don't need my slave to sit on the floor to know it's my slave. More than that, I usually have planned things for our evenings that require the slave to be active, not sitting at my feet. For example, when we are Dining In, the slave will frequently be dressed in a tuxedo, a dinner jacket, or tails. Sitting at my feet on the floor is incongruous with the mood I wish established.

That said, when a kink couple has joined us for a semi-formal dinner, I prefer the slave to sit on the floor at my feet whether I'm sitting in a chair or on the couch. This is a powerful indicator of relative status and correctly reflects the way we live.

Table manners

Table manners reflect what you've learned about the art of dining. Good manners show respect for others at your table. People's views about what is and is not proper at the dinner table reflect their upbringing and their aspirations. Some people simply don't care how they hold their utensils; some people willingly use their fingers to eat their food.

As it is my intention to set a particular mood in my home, I expect my slave to follow my lead in its dining manners and habits.

- Dining In: My slave is expected to be intimately familiar with dining etiquette and use that knowledge daily for all our meals. (Section Three describes our specific dining protocols; general etiquette protocols are provided in the supplements.)

- Dining Out: We enjoy dining out and have developed the following protocols.

  ○ The slave will only speak directly to the waitstaff upon Master's specific instructions.

  ○ The slave will convey any meal preferences to Master, who will communicate that order directly to the waitstaff.

  ○ The slave and Master will always share a single main course: slave will eat whatever Master chooses to eat.

- ○ The slave will taste food before adding any seasoning. In the world of business, seasoning your food without tasting it suggests that you reach conclusions without assessing facts.

- ○ If the slave does not like the food or the way it was prepared, slave is to keep this information to itself unless a food-safety issue is involved. I *do not* like food discussed at the table. We are dining out to have a good time, not to discuss the meal. If slave does not like a food, this dislike will not be noticeable to others, especially Master.

Service

This part provides a high-level view of the house protocols. The third section of this Manual provides ample details. Bits and pieces that relate to service will pop up throughout this Manual, but here I've laid them out in a short, straight path to help you understand the details provided in Section Three.

In the broadest sense, unless we are both working on the relationship, neither of us is truly *in* the relationship. By extension, I expect you, as my slave, always to be serving the *idea* or *concept* of the relationship. There are certain proxies that demonstrate the degree of the slave's commitment to our relationship. So far as I am concerned, they include the following:

- • Anticipatory service: Master expects slave to learn my likes, dislikes, needs, and wants in order to be able to provide anticipatory service. The slave is not to wait to be directed: if slave see something that needs doing, it is to act. I've attached an article on anticipatory service so you'll understand what I mean.

- Responsive service: When Master directs slave to serve, it will do so immediately, willingly, and with a positive attitude. Any cerebral or emotional conflicts or issues will be expressed immediately.

- Competent service: Master prefers macro management over micro management. When I tell slave to do something, I assume it is capable of figuring out how to do it. "Competence" is a threshold requirement to be my slave. The slave is expected to ask for clarification if it doesn't know some fact or process. *Not knowing how to do something is not an excuse for poor execution*.

- Chastity service: Chastity is enforced at all times. The slave may only cum with permission. This includes times when we are playing sexually together. You must ask permission to cum whether touching yourself, being touched, or engaging in oral or vaginal penetration. I may direct you to masturbate occasionally or on a regular basis. If you cum without prior permission, you disappoint me and I'll decide how to handle it based on the circumstances. You are advised not to withhold from me information concerning this topic.

- Physical appearance: The slave's physical appearance and bearing communicate confidence. Confidence connects with one's outward appeal.

As I prefer to be with a slave that appeals to me, physical exercise and snappy clothing are part of your service obligations.

What "service" means to me

Not only do I care the kind of service I'm receiving from you as my slave, I care how you execute your service. To set the tone, here is a quote from Butchmann's:

> After a slave is in a PRESENTING position, it pauses to feel the presence of their slavery. It is important for the slave to take the needed time for this—to feel the strength and dedication of their slavery, to let the rush and static of the outside world subside, and to find the peace of its slavery before addressing the Master.
>
> The Butchmann's Experience
> *Feeling your slavery*

In the spirit of that quote, I have designed some protocols for specific actions. They are these:

- Walking: When serving food or drink, slave is reminded to follow the concept of effortless technique. Approach slowly and with grace. Specifically, slave is not to appear hurried: slave is to focus and remain present.

- Presenting drinks other than at Table: Before handing the a beverage to Master, slave will assume a Full Present position and, with deliberation, kiss the edge of the glass with eyes lowered and present the gift with a slow and deliberate gesture, holding the glass in the palm of its hands (that are on top of one-another at the palms). Note: the intent is that slave **focus** its attention on the moment; that slave demonstrate cognizance of its status and the importance of the *ceremony of service.*

- <u>Rising from Full Present</u>: Following Master's release, slave will roll backwards on the tips of its shoes in order then to rise to a standing position in one single, fluid motion without having to stabilize itself in the process.

- <u>Withdrawing from Master's presence</u>: The slave will then stand and bow (demonstrating *intentionality)*, step backward, turn and leave. Note: slave will **not** turn its back on Master until taking a purposeful step backward.

House maintenance

I wish the house to be sparkly at all times. I wish the kitchen to be spotless and uncluttered. I wish the living room to be as tidy and "correct" when I come home from work as it would be if guests were arriving any minute. I wish the pianos dusted and polished and the dining room table formally set.

Dining

We will have two levels of dining: casual and semi-formal. Casual means that we will sit on the couch with our dinner service set up on the coffee table. Occasionally, we will stream a movie during dinner. We still use china, crystal, silver, and cloth napkins, but we may not have showered and changed clothes. We do not eat at Table unless we've showered and dressed.

Semi-formal means that we're dressed in fetish wear of some sort. "Of some sort" can vary from vampish to gowns for Master and from clownish to tails for slave.

Dining at Table (Dining In), is far more for me than simply eating dinner. Dining In is a ceremony; it's a ritualized experience. It involves special clothing, stylized protocols that include sexual touching, and paced eating.[28] I expect the slave to exhibit exemplary table manners and also be able to maintain interesting dinner conversation.

Let me focus on "Table conversation:" the slave's job is to entertain me. slave is welcome to summarize important news, explore interesting words, or be prepared to discuss concepts and ideas. Certain topics are off-limits once we're at Table. I'm not interested in hearing about the slave's work life or about any of our friends or associates. I'm not interested in hearing about drama of any sort. We had ample time to speak casually: we're not dining casually when we're Dining In.

Establishing the mood
At night, the entire house is to exude an amber glow, con-sistent from room to room. The slave will adjust light lev-els as soon as it is dark enough to know how to set them. The slave is responsible for monitoring and adjusting light

levels to maintain that effect. Fluorescent kitchen overhead and under-counter lights shall be used very sparingly and turned off once we begin our cocktail hour.

It is Master's intent that we treat "Dining In" as an opportunity to express gratitude for our friends and for the gift of being able to live as we do. We celebrate that we live in the age we do, are in good health, and have the amazing good fortune of living in a country that enables us to live as we do.

Also, we are celebrating that we are similarly idiosyncratic and think it's cool to dress up and listen to Frank Sinatra and his cronies play for us while a vicious thunderstorm rages around us, triggering our DJ lights to change the ambient color of the dining room / living room.[29]

Formality

The slave is expected to support Master's preference for fetishize dining. Even when we're sitting in the living room and dining casually from the cofwfee table, the slave remains responsible for maintaining the feel of the overall experience.[30]

Considering how stylized our dinners have become, I have directed the slave to prepare a handout to serve as a guide to guests. Master is aware that those receiving such a guide may think it a little odd, but I suspect that everybody who knows us well enough to be invited to dinner knows we're a little odd. Anyway, nobody likes surprises, particularly when having dinner at someone's house.

Only Master will send this sheet. The slave is not to reveal its existence in advance.

Daily service

I'm now going to move from the general concept of service to describe areas of service throughout the day. Specific protocols for most of these areas are covered in the third section of this Manual. Some of the finer points are covered under "Sparkly service" in Section Four.

Typical Morning Protocol

The slave is responsible for preparing Master's morning tea and serving it 15 minutes before Master is to leave for work. If Master so requests, slave will also prepare Master's lunch.

Unless the slave has some residual house straightening to do, Master and slave will leave together for the workday. If the slave feels it does not have time to totally restore the house in the morning, it must explain this before Master leaves.

Daily contact protocol

During the day slave will be available for Master by phone, text, or IM at all times or provide prior explanation why slave expects to be unavailable.

- The slave is to text Master when work demands render it unavailable for some period.

- The slave shall keep Master apprised of any out-of-building periods, particularly around lunch time (as we may be able to link up during that time).

At or about 1:00p each day Master will text slave so they may speak for a few minutes. As Master may not use a phone at the office, this is our only chance to communicate until the workday ends. If convenient, Master will text the slave once in the car and heading home so the slave knows how much prep time remains before Master arrives.

During one of these conversations, Master will notify slave of Masters after-work needs and desires as well as the expected direction of the evening activities. Similarly, if the slave has any particular suggestions for the evening, it will communicate those.

slave's tasks upon arriving home from work
As the slave usually arrives home almost 90 minutes before Master, it uses this time to prepare the house for our Evening. There are many stages in this process.

If not left in perfect condition that morning; the slave washes anything left over from the prior night (commonly some wine glasses), puts dishes away (that had been drying in the dishwasher racks), removes anything that might have spent the night on a kitchen counter surface, and sprays/cleans the counters. If the floor has not been cleaned within the past 48 hours, the slave will now do so.

After preparing the kitchen, the slave checks the entire house for clutter, putting everything away that is not in its rightful place.

The slave will take care of as much yard work as possible before Master arrives. At a minimum, the slave uses a forced-air blowing machine to clear leaves and debris from in front of our door and the walkway leading from Master's car to the front door. If we intend to use the back deck that evening, the slave will also blow it clear of leaves and debris.

If the slave did yard work, it will then shower and change into its house uniform. If no yard work, then it is free to work on its computer until Master arrives.

Early evening ritual[31]

If I have texted my arrival time, I expect my slave to greet me at the door in its house uniform. If I simply walk in, I expect my slave to assume Full Present position the moment it lays eyes on me. However, there is an exception to this: if my arms are full, the slave will take what I proffer so I may continue into the kitchen or the bedroom to put away the remainder of what I am carrying.

I require the slave not to interact with me until I specifically recognize it. I need a period of quiet. This will take a minimum of 30 minutes, and more likely 45-60 minutes. The slave is released to do what it needs to during this period.

If I have texted in advance, I expect Port and cheese and crackers to be awaiting me on the coffee table. If I have not texted in advance, I'll now tell you whether I wish a snack.

If I have not already told you what to prepare for dinner, I'll now tell you. Sometimes I'll tell you that I intend to prepare dinner; other times I'll tell you that we're going out to dinner.

slave's tasks during this quiet time

This is the time when the slave turns on all house lights to their correct brightness.[32] Once complete, the house glows with a rich orange color. Depending upon the time of year, the slave will either set and light a fire in the fireplace, or light the candles in the fireplace.

During this same cycle (lighting the fire or the candles) slave will lock the front door and turn on the front porch light. Finally, the slave will turn on the colorful back-yard Holiday lights that remain year-round in our trees and bushes.

Master returns to living room

Once Master returns to the living room, the slave will use standard serving protocols to present Master's drink and to prepare such snacks as Master had requested be ready at this time.

This portion of the evening is intended as a relaxed period of interaction, a time for casual descriptions of the high and low aspects of Master's and slave's day. Depending upon the day of the week, we may:

- Prepare to Dine In for a sensual evening;
- Use some time for work we may need to address;
- Prepare to go out dancing;
- Decide to go out for dinner; or
- Set up for a massage or play session.

This is the time for each of us to tell the other of things noteworthy that happened that day. As a general rule, 7pm marks the separation between social time and showering and dressing for Dinner. At this time, Master indicates the level of formality for the balance of the evening. This is explained in more detail in Section Three.

Evening ground rules

Our evenings are private time devoted to celebrating our relationship. Unless there is some unusual circumstance, this is "protected time."

- <u>Phones</u>: Phones will be turned off by 6pm.

- <u>eMails</u>: The slave may not check eMails or do any other work on its computer unless specifically granted permission to do so.

- <u>Showering</u>: The slave will shower and, per the schedule previously specified, groom its mustache and beard.

- <u>Dress</u>: There are three general levels of dress:[33]

  - House uniform for the slave, house dress for Master

  - Playful (may be slutty or outrageous)

  - Formal (Military mess dress or white dinner jacket or tux or tails)

Last steps before bed

Before beginning bedroom protocols, there is a final house check. The slave will verify that all doors and windows are locked, and that all interior and exterior lights are turned off.

The slave will also ensure that all extension cords used that night for play have been put away. The slave will move furniture, as needed, to ensure an unimpeded path from the bedroom both to the front and back doors in case of a nighttime emergency. The slave will also verify that its wallet and keys are in their designated place—again, in case of emergency.

Once complete, the slave is ready to begin bedtime protocols.

I wish the slave first to rearrange the pillows, turn down the sheet/blanket on my side of the bed and fluff my pillow. Next, it will make two piles of our evening medications and bring my pills to me. It will assume a Full Present position and offer the pills from one hand and a glass $2/3$ filled with water in the other hand. Once finished, I will release the slave to take its own medications.

The slave will verify that its cell phone is silenced and that the correct morning alarms are set.

Once in bed, the slave is free to use its cell phone to catch up on the news while I finish playing a game or two on my iPad. Once I'm done, the two of us will play a few games of Word Warp before turning out the lights.

Integrating Concepts and Action

Standing orders
Chain of command
slave serves Master. All decisions are made in this light. The only exception is stipulated in Rule Two.

Levels of protocol

We are to live in a fairly high level of formal protocol. I will inform the slave when I wish a lower protocol level.

The slave will speak in third-person, address me formally, and remain silent unless addressed. If it wishes to speak, it will make that wish known by body posture, not by interrupting my silence.

We will use no level of protocol around minors. For all other times there are three levels of protocol; each builds upon the other:

- Social Protocol: Unless utterly socially inappropriate, the slave refers to me as "Master" but has no other language restriction. The slave is free to speak and ask questions without limitation. The slave may walk arm-in-arm with me, and in all other ways appear to be part of a "vanilla" couple.

- Low Protocol: Low Protocol is used when out in public (as in a mall or at a restaurant). Walking and standing protocols are invoked. The slave will not sit until I've been seated. The slave will arise each time I get up. The slave will ask permission if it needs to go somewhere.

- High Protocol: All formal protocols are invoked—especially the *languaging* and *attending* protocols. The slave's sole purpose is to please me and make my life easier; slave is *not* free to engage in discourse with me or anyone else. The slave is expected to think of itself as my personal assistant and remain *highly alert* to any logistical issue or problem that may need to be solved (such as reminding me of someone's name or taking a proffered business card).

Agreements

For "things that matter," Master operates in the world of follow-through. Following through on something promised reflects on one's personal honor. Agreements fit into this discussion.[34]

Agreements have four components:

- State the offer/acceptance; (I agree...)

- Specify the general item to be done; (to wash the outside of the car...)

- List conditions of satisfaction—be clear about the level of activity; (...so that all the dirt and tar are completely removed and no water spots remain...)

- Specify the time frame; (...within the next two hours.).

The modification of any aspect of an Agreement *must* occur BEFORE the agreement is accepted or as soon as the need for modification becomes apparent.

If slave finds it may be unable to complete an Agreement on time, it will contact Master and discuss the situation before the deadline arrives.

Master recognizes that my slave occasionally agrees to things it really does not intend to do in the hopes that I'll forget about it. Master encourages slave to change this behavior, as it is manipulative and passive-aggressive and does not advance our relationship.

Failure to keep an agreement will carry consequences.

Time commitments

Time is important in this Household. Time commitments represent daily opportunities to keep your word. They are a form of Agreement.

If slave has been told an arrival or departure time, Master expects that time to be precisely honored. Disrespecting time issues that cause me to have to wait for my slave carry consequences

My slave is to be on time (or early) for events and activities. I have observed that my slave does not handle multiple concurrent tasks very well. Since "focus and mindfulness" are core values within our relationship, I have settled upon this protocol: When slave begins a task, it will stay focused on that task and not to begin another task until the original task is completed. For example: when slave enters the kitchen to refresh Master's drink, slave is to return and serve Master's drink before interjecting any other task, such as fixing itself a drink or a snack or tidying the kitchen.

If I, as Master, have told someone that I will arrive at a certain time, tardiness by my slave will NOT cause me to be late to that meeting. If my slave is not ready to leave on time, I will leave without it. I run a Leather household that lives by HILT standards: Honor, Integrity, Loyalty, and Trust. The slave is not by boyfriend or my partner, it is my slave: its value correlates to the quality of its service.

Communication issues

Corrections in public

The slave will not correct a Family member in public. All corrections are conducted in private. Violation of this Protocol will have dramatic consequences, as it demonstrates that I, as Master, have failed to train you appropriately. Such behavior communicates disharmony and lack of respect. It undermines our relationship and demonstrates poor manners.

Direct questions from another

When slave doesn't know the answer to a direct question, it is to:

- Admit it. No one is expected to know everything. The slave will gain more "points" for admitting it-doesn't know something than trying to concoct or guess at the answer. The slave will be sensitive to and avoid the arrogance of chauvinistic *male answer syndrome*.[35]

- Find out the answer and tell the person. The actual phrasing of the response depends upon the setting. In a general sense, the slave is to say that it doesn't know the answer and will do some research, after which it will report its findings. The slave's formal response to Master in this case is as follows: "Master, this slave does not know the full answer right now. With permission it will research this issue and provide an informed answer. Within what time frame does Master wish this additional information?" This is a case wherein the way the slave handles follow-up reflects upon me, my management style, and your integrity.

When slave DOES know the answer to a direct question but fears that the person asking the question won't like the answer, consider using a phrase such as, "It seems to me I read somewhere..." then give the correct answer. This leaves open the possibility that the slave may not be remembering the fact precisely. It softens the blow.

Humor/jokes

Master enjoys a good joke and loves hearing amusing stories. However, the slave will not relate jokes or stories that denigrate a person or class of people (women, blondes, old people, ethnic groups).

Conversational ease

Group settings sometimes make me feel uncomfortable. Not only do I have control issues, but also I can become claustrophobic with many people in a small area. Because of this, my slave will closely monitor my comfort when we're with others. If we are speaking with people and the slave notices that I've become unusually silent, it will take control of the conversation and discretely ask whether I need to leave. If we are alone, I'll instruct it to remove me from the area. This will need to be executed very quickly. In order that the slave always has something cogent to say if I falter in a social conversation, it is instructed to remain current with world and national news in order to interject something that makes sense.

Honesty in verbal communication

I have sometimes noticed that my slave will agree to do things for others that the slave would prefer not to do, but does not know how to decline politely. I don't mind others making very minor use of my slave; I *do* object to my slave being placed in the position of feeling it has to accept a task that is time-consuming without having discussed it with me privately. In this regard, the slave will adhere to the following protocol:

> My slave is personally responsible for living in integrity. It will not adjust its integrity to help satisfy the needs of others. It will prioritize as follows: the needs of the relationship come first, the slave's own needs come second, others' needs follow. If necessary, the slave will receive guidance and scripting from Master. If it feels it is being put on the spot, it is to say: "While I may be able to help, I need to discuss this with Master."

Conflicts of opinion in social conversations

It may happen that we are in a social setting and someone states an opinion that my slave knows substantially opposes my opinion. My slave is directed not to become verbally aggressive. My slave is reminded that there is no value in *being right* or proving someone wrong. If slave is asked for its specific opinion on this (or some other controversial) matter and cannot avoid answering, it is to reply: "With due respect, in this matter of opinion my experience has been to the contrary." While not encouraged to do so, it may voice its opinion, preferably backed up by facts. My slave is to avoid controversy whenever possible. The slave is reminded that each of us creates our own interpretation of the world around us and the opinions of others are likely to be valid in the context of their reality.[36]

Social gaffes

As my slave is twenty years my senior, is a sociologist with a broad range of etiquette training and international travel, and has a personal interest in the mechanics of social interaction, I'm going to insert a protocol that permits the slave to act without my guidance:

> If the slave believes Master is making (or has made) a social gaffe, slave is to intervene and neutralize the situation to the extent it can. Later, and privately, the slave will explain what the slave thought Master had missed. The slave is cautioned that with its Asperger condition, it's unlikely to be more sensitive than Master to social innuendo. I will also point out that I am able to process several conversation levels at once. What you may interpret as a social gaffe may actually be my response to some part of the conversation of which the slave is unaware.

With some trepidation, I'll include this unusual protocol as a form of a Rule Two exception permitting independent action. I'll do this on the grounds that being out of my social depth is a form of mental illness: I must have been out of my mind to have placed myself into this situation. Yes, I'm joking, sort of. But, you had better be very careful if you are going to take over a social interaction in a way that reveals a social protocol breach on my part. If I feel offended by your intercession, I will walk out, and the consequences will be extremely unpleasant.

Behavior in public
Doors and Elevators
slave will open all doors and elevators (and any related apparatus) for Master, and will follow once Master has passed through.

- Doors: When there is an outer and inner door, slave will open the first door to let Master pass, then enter and—as Master waits—open the second door. Should a third person be present with us, the general concept is that slave is Master's *Personal Assistant* and must remain "attached" to Master at all times. That means that the when the person following Master enters the "between-door" space, the slave will now have to walk around (or in front of) that person in order to open the door for Master *and then follow Master through the second door.* (Note: if the other person has more Leather rank than Master, then the slave will continue to hold the second door for that person to pass through. The assumption, here, is that

that other person is in an ongoing conversation with Master and the slave is thus helping to keep that conversation running smoothly.)

- Elevators: Once an elevator door opens, the slave will move its arm or body in such a way as to ensure the elevator doors remain open as Master enters. The slave will be the last person to enter the elevator and will depress the elevator buttons, as needed. The slave is going to have to read the particular situation to decide whether it will follow directly behind Master upon arriving at our designated floor or will hold the elevator door open until everyone has exited. If we are at a protocol-sensitive conference, the slave will follow directly behind Master so long as we are the senior couple exiting. If not, the slave and I will defer to the more senior Leatherperson and exit behind them.

Walking

Unless directed otherwise, the slave will walk on the side closest to the street. When Master so indicates, the slave will "link" with Master. The "linking protocol" takes advantage of our 9"-10" height difference when Master is in heels: the slave will put an arm around Master's waist and Master will droop her arm behind the slave's head and over its shoulder. The slave will match pace in such a way that each of our inside legs move forward at the same time.

When walking through a crowded room, the slave will walk in front of Master to clear a path. This also serves to maintain a comfort zone so Master does not feel crowded.

Driving

slave will open the car door for Master, secure Master's seatbelt, assure that Master is seated correctly as protocol dictates, and close the door.

When slave is driving, it is expected to behave as *chauffeur* and perform all the customary roles expected of such a position. The slave is admonished to drive in a conservative and defensive manner, particularly attending to the distance maintained from the car immediately in front of us. The slave is never to be the first car into an intersection when the light turns green.

slave is not permitted to use its cell phone while driving. This includes opening any driving-assistance programs. The slave is to launch these programs when the car is not moving. When we are together, Master will launch the programs.

Forms of address

Following the guidelines set forth in the Butchmann's protocols, my slave will address me as "Master" as often as seems suitable to me.

When we are in High Protocol, I expect slave to use "Master" in virtually every sentence (e.g.: "Master, would you like the blinds drawn?").

Only my slave may call me "Master." It is a title reserved for him alone as it describes our personal dynamic.

Outside Friends

Relations with outside friends

("Outside" means outside of Master's Leather Family with this slave.)

Master will respect slave's work life, but will decide about slave's friends individually, based on their support of our relationship and of the slave, itself. The slave is responsible for conveying any potential conflicts between Master's instructions/rules and anything that goes on away from Master's presence.

Master encourages slave to develop and maintain friendships with others, whether male, female, Dom/me, slave, or submissive. it will advise Master when it would like to invite someone to dinner (or go out with them socially). If Master agrees, we will check our calendars and coordinate an appropriate time.

The slave is to speak with me in advance concerning ongoing relationships with others. I will rarely deny outside friendships, but I want to discuss the possible impact such friendships might have upon our own relationship. Specifically, I want to consider my slave's level of proposed interaction with respect to our established rules/protocols. Without exception, all sexual relations with others will include safer sex practices.

The slave may be permitted to spend time with acquaintances including dinners, movie outings, camping, etc. At

Master's pleasure, these occasions may range from hours to several days in duration. The slave remains "on duty" during these occasions, remaining in full compliance with our Contract and all protocols pertaining to personal behavior, dress, and activities.

The slave will maintain these friendships as secondary relationships with the power and position a secondary relationship holds.[37] The slave will not put the needs of a friend above Master's (or slave's) needs—whether a physical need or an emotional one.

Being loaned out overnight

In rare instances, the slave may be loaned out to learn a skill or to provide some practical service. Special rules govern slave at these times.

- All activity expected of the slave will be pre-negotiated between Master and the person to whom slave is being loaned.

- Master will always know the slave's physical location. If the slave is changing locations, it will inform Master.

- If sexual intercourse is involved, this MUST be pre-negotiated with me and condoms must be used.

- Fingernails, teeth, or bite marks, are prohibited. There will be no marks from sexual passion left on my slave.

Service to another Master, Domme, or vanilla female

At times, slave might have an opportunity to serve another Master or Dom/me. In those cases, its behavior and actions are governed by the rules and protocols set forth in this Manual.

If the other Master or Dom/me asks the slave to perform some activity that is restricted or prohibited by the spirit or letter of the contents of this Manual, the slave will dutifully inform them that it is not permitted to comply with their wishes. If the situation is repeated or persists, slave will inform Master at once in person, by phone, or by text (if Master is unreachable by phone). The slave will be forceful enough to make the needs of our Family and Contract clear and will be VERY CAREFUL not to bring disrespect to our Family through its actions.

The slave may not touch others without my permission. This covers all forms of BDSM and sexual "play." If play has not been negotiated and they wish you to play, slave will direct them to speak with Master before discussing it further. If there is someone with whom the slave is interested in playing, slave will **first** discuss this with Master, who will approach them to determine their level of interest. In some cases, Master may direct the slave to negotiate directly. From time to time, Master may direct the slave to play with others whom Master feels are safe and competent players. The slave does not have the authority to refuse a scene that Master has negotiated. Play with others will be subject to Master's terms and conditions.

Master is to be copied on all email correspondence. In this way, everybody knows that Master is fully informed of the slave's other relationship. The slave will provide a detailed briefing when there are private meetings between my slave and another Master, Dom/me, or vanilla female. Master will not pry into details of an approved relationship, however the relationship will be curtailed at my first sense of secrecy. If slave has been asked to keep an action with another female "between the two of them," slave is to inform this other female that it will not be able to comply. There are no exceptions to this rule. The slave will be transparent in all its dealings with others.

Unless I have arranged or pre-approved your play, you may not play* at a play party from which I am absent. This is a hard-limit at the level of Contract, and there simply are no exceptions. (* Note: "Play" means to touch or be touched with sexual or intimate intent using any body part or sm tool/toy.)

The slave does not have *prima facae* permission to maintain any kind of contact with the Host. The Host would have to contact me for ongoing contact with my slave. Should the Host contact slave without permission, slave will forward such communication directly to me without replying.

"Thank-You" Notes

The slave will write a formal "thank you" note to the Host within 24 hours of the visit. As usual, Master will be "copied" on all emails.

Section Two Footnotes
Footnotes 22-37

22 At a High Protocol event, Masters would only speak with other Masters: slaves would be expected to remain in service mode. They may speak quietly amongst themselves so long as they do not disturb their Masters. Individual protocols may require some visiting slaves to remain on-point with their Masters. In other cases, the visiting slaves will be seconded to my slave to assist with the overall service for the evening.

23 My slave is the author of "Squirms, Screams, and Squirts: Handbook for going from great sex to extraordinary sex," and puts on workshops and demos on "How to Pleasure a Lady" and "Playing Hard with a Lady" and has a swingers background.

24 IML, CLAW, MAL and some Master/slave conferences.

25 Greeting rituals between Leathermen and between Leathermen and submissives/slaves are one of the defining characteristics of the Leather Lifestyle. When two Leathermen meet, the senior Leatherman extends their hand to the junior Leatherman. Often, there is a pregnant moment while the two people try to sort out who is senior. In my slave's case, his rank as an author and well-known presenter causes this protocol to be "softer" than would otherwise be the case. Many senior Leatherfolk come up and initiate conversation as though speaking with someone of equal rank. If the setting is formal, they introduce him as "Dr. Bob."

96

26 Our relationship status is often confused. Because I dress "high-femme," am much taller (and 20 years younger) than my slave, (and because he is so well-known in the BDSM and Leather worlds), most people assume that he is the Master and I am something else. We've had many instances—particularly when our relationship was fairly new—where people would chat away with slave and totally ignore me. It was an uncomfortable moment when he would introduce me as his Owner. To avoid that, he now introduces me immediately as his Owner.

27 slave will not leave Masters side unless I've requested something and will not seek out others to speak with them. However, if someone approaches us to speak with me, slave is permitted to second Master in the conversation.

28 Each of us monitors the pace at which the other is eating so we complete our meal at the same time. That said, if Master is clearly finished with her meal, the slave—by definition—is also finished with its meal and immediately offers to escort Master to the living room.

29 The loud thunder triggers a little strobe light, so we even get our flicker of bright white lightning. The thunder also triggers a sound-activated DJ light that changes suddenly from solid red to blue to green to yellow and various in-between shades. That illuminates our mantle on the opposite was and whatever mobile we have pinned to the ceiling some three inches in front of the fireplace wall—above the mantle.

30   Let me describe the house. We have a largish living room, about 15' x 30'. While the house came with a dining room, we're using that room as our library and for the Yamaha Disclavier piano. A "Disclaviar piano" is the modern version of a player piano. While it can be played as a standard acoustic piano, it can also be played from a computer floppy disk inserted into it's own computer. Our dining room table is on one side of the fireplace, our couch and coffee table are on the other side. We dine and play sexually in the living room.

      We use lighting to establish ambiance. One of the first things we do when we move to another house or apartment is to change the light switches from simple on/off to dimmers in all rooms we use during the evening. In our current house, we've changed out every switch except in the guest bedroom and guest bath.

31   A ritual is any practice or pattern of behavior regularly performed in a set manner. But, it is a ritual because it has spiritual significance for the performer. Otherwise, it the behavior would be just a habit. This is why rituals can get a bad reputation; many people participating in a ritual are not involving their spirit, and therefore are only going through the motions. Because of this, a lot of people tend to overlook the value of ritual.

32   "Turning on the lights" is actually quite a production. All lights in our home are on dimmers. Most, but not all, are preset. The music room requires adjusting

two lights. The library requires adjusting three lights. The kitchen also requires two lights. The living room requires five adjustments on one side of the room and three adjustments on the other side. The bedroom requires adjustments to the overhead lights, the individual lights on either side of our bed and the light on one bureau. There is also a decorative art piece with a battery-operated light inside it that must be turned on. The bathroom light needs to be turned on and its level adjusted. This process takes over five minutes to complete.

33   We use clothing as a key element in what is called "state change." (See Neuro-Linguistic Programming for more information.) That is, by changing from our work clothes to something else, we are visibly "not at work." For us, *changing clothes* helps us enter our own magical world. It changes our moods. Since my slave works in a professional office (black suit pants, long-sleeved shirt, suit coat or blazer) it is to change into its House Uniform as part of the mental adjustment back to its slave headspace.

34   "Keeping one's word" is a core concept within the Leather culture. If a Leatherman says something will be done, you can be assured that it will be.

35   "Male answer syndrome" occurs when you ask most men a question. Whether or not they know the correct answer, they will produce an answer. It is culturally expected that men know the answers to things.

36 Bob's dominance can surface when we are speaking with people who don't understand our power dynamic and assume that he's in charge of the relationship. Unless he is careful, he can get caught up in the conversation and stray onto topics where our opinions differ. Because of this, Bob is to listen and respond to people in a neutral manner, neither agreeing nor disagreeing. That leaves me the option of leading the response or asking Bob to reply to a specific point.

37 In order to remain fully informed about the nature of relationships with actual or potential play partners, I expect Bob to share all emails or texts with me.

Section Three
Dinner Service

I have a number of reasons for having chosen *formal service* as your path as my slave. With Asperger Syndrome, you thrive on routine. Because of your personal upbringing, you thrive on formality. Because of your aesthetic tastes, you like the house kept particularly clean and tidy. I certainly enjoy the fruits of your labor. I've never been around anyone who keeps their house as I wish and as you do. Even though this is your protocol manual, I want to thank you for doing this: it's like coming home to a resort, and it frees me to concentrate on other aspects of life and living.

As you were born in 1944 to parents of means, you were raised in an upscale version of what we now call the "1950s household model" of structured relationships. Your father was in charge, your mother deferred to him, and you got dressed up a little bit to go out shopping, at which time your mother wore white gloves. I get it. As depicted in movies set in that time, your family gathered together for the evening meal. You have told me that you were not allowed to wear blue jeans to dinner, that you wore light blue denim slacks.

You have also told me that you are used to being required to know and use traditional formal table manners and that your father used these family gatherings as an opportunity to expound on learned topics, mostly about science or history. To build on your background, quite similar to mine in many ways as my own father was raised this way and maintained certain aspects within his own house, I have chosen to support the ways your background plays out in your adult life.

It is my wish that we bring formality to our time together in the evenings. It is my wish that you bring humor, stories, history, or current news to our dinnertime together. It is my wish that you have prepared this material beforehand in order that our time at Table has focus.

This part of your Manual is devoted to dinner service. Although you already know most of this, I've written it out in order to refine and polish some aspects of your service. Also, I invested a lot of time and trouble with this part of your Manual in order to solidify what I expect.

About the Table

The Table is always set

My slave is to reset the table each night before coming to bed. If this is not feasible, reset the table in the morning before going to work. If slave was unable to reset the table before leaving for work, you are to send me a text that lets me know how/when you will rectify this situation.

Here are some specific guidelines:

- Polish the silver at least once a week.

- Using the polishing cloths, polish glasses and plates before replacing them on the table.

- Each place setting will consist of a charger plate and a dinner plate, a water glass and a red wine glass, knife and spoon on right, salad and dinner forks on the left of the plates. This is the default setting arrangement.

- The napkins will be folded using a design appropriate for tucking the salad and dinner forks into the fold at the bottom edge of the napkin.

- Selecting either the black or the cream-colored tablecloth and napkin set unless specifically directed otherwise.

- If replacing the tablecloth, leave the "silence pad" on the table. Note: When we're dining "full-formal," use our bright-white tablecloth over the silence pad.

- If somehow changed, restore the centerpiece as it was arranged the prior night. Master designs the centerpieces.

- When we have company, the slave will prepare place cards and place them in their holders. slave is responsible that all guest name spellings have been verified and that these cards are correctly placed in relation to the guest's rank. If more than one couple is joining us, Master will provide the Order of Precedence sheet with a seating diagram.[38]

- Perform a final place-setting check before starting dinner preparations. Specifically, make sure plates, glasses, and cutlery are correctly aligned and that cutlery not needed for this specific meal have been removed.

- At this point, the slave will know whether the meal calls for red or white wine. Should the meal require white wine, it will now change the red-wine glasses for white-wine glasses and replace the wine caddy for the wine chiller.

slave is to use the detailed "Pre-dinner Checklist" to ensure that the entire house is prepared correctly when we Dine In or have company for dinner. (See supplementary material).

Table setup details

We'll use chargers to add color and texture to my table. Each charger (topped with the dinner plate) will be centered between the cutlery, each place setting equidistant from those around it. The rest of the components used to set a formal table will be set with the charger plate in mind. The slave will use its butlers' stick to verify measurements and alignments. Attend, particularly, to the alignment of water and wine glasses with respect to adjacent place settings. When in doubt, refer to place-setting diagrams included in the supplementary material.

While I prefer charger plates remain throughout our meals, there is an exception to that rule. If we're serving a bowl of soup or melon balls as the first course, the entire setting (charger plate and soup or melon bowls) will be removed before presenting the next course. If we're following the "soup or melon balls" clearing protocol, I will inform you whether you will be bringing a clean charger and dinner plate set to Table after clearing the charger and bowls or whether you'll be bringing a charger plate first and then serving a plated meal on a dinner plate.

Water and wine glasses are to be polished before being placed on the table. While your routine protocol for washing glasses calls for them to be polished after each use, glasses used for guests are taken from our breakfront. The slave is to polish all glasses and dishes before setting them on the table. Similarly, the slave is to use the polishing cloths for all silverware taken from their storage drawer before using them for guests. If the slave detects any tarnish (for example, on fork tines), slave is to tidy the piece with silver polish, rewash and dry with the polishing cloths.

Stemware is placed above and to the right side of the plate. If more than one drink is served to each person, position each piece of glassware along a line slanting slightly towards the dinner knife. Stemware is arranged in order of use, starting from the right. I wish the water glass to be the first glass, then wine glasses arranged according to the order that they will be used with the various courses.

As an example, if we're serving a fruit or fish dish followed by a meat dish followed by dessert, then the order of glasses would be:

- Water
- White wine
- Red wine
- Dessert wine[39]

(Note: There is an alternate protocol for placing the dessert wine glasses. Rather than including dessert wine glasses with other glasses when the table is first set, they can be brought out just before serving the plated dessert. Master prefers this serving style. It simplifies the look of the table, as used plates and glasses will already have been cleared.)

Logistical details
Serving wine

While enologists recommend serving different ages of red and white wines at specific (and different) temperatures, the clave will serve red wines at room temperature. They are to be opened to breathe 30 minutes prior to serving. If we are serving a white wine, the slave will be certain to chill sufficient bottles.[40]

When pouring wine, slave will add a quarter-bottle twist as it raises the bottle to a more upright position from the pouring position to avoid dripping wine onto the tablecloth. When we have company for dinner, the slave will wrap the neck of the wine bottle in the napkin designated for that purpose.

When Dining In alone, if a drop of wine or piece of food lands on the tablecloth, slave is immediately to remove the food/liquid, clean the spill, and restart whatever service was interrupted by the event. Notes: 1.) To "clean the spill" may mean using a wine-specific stain remover right then. Master doesn't want a red wine stain to set. 2.) "Restart" does not mean "resume," it means *start over from the beginning*. slave can only learn perfect service through perfect practice.

Walking around the table to serve
The slave will walk counter-clockwise around the dining room table. There are two reasons for this. First, it brings consistence to the table service; second, it lines the slave up correctly for serving dishes from the left side of someone seated at Table.[41]

Regardless of slight differences in service protocols in highly formal dinners, it is our standing protocol to serve foods from left and remove plates from the right. Liquids, whether water or wine, are to be served and refilled from the right.

When serving a plated dish, the slave will take care to place the dish so the meat or fish is in the 4-5 o'clock position. Vegetables and sides will be roughly in the 9-12 o'clock position.

The slave will enter the dining area and walk counter-clockwise around the table to deliver Master's plate. The slave will place the meal on the charger plate from an Honor Present position. slave will pay particular attention to place the dinner plate on the charger plate making as little noise as possible.

Plating protocols

The slave is to be mindful about how it places each type of food on the plate: Dining is an intimate service ritual between us that has great meaning. The look of the plate is as important as the way the food tastes. Master prefers the slave to be artistic when plating a meal. it is to decorate the plate with colorful foods, such as candied apples, parsley, and love notes. You can gain a lot of slave points for including a love note with the dinner service.

There is one final step required when preparing plated food. This step provides that "extra touch" that leads to sparkly service: the slave will wipe any spilled juices or seasonings from the outer edge (or lip) of the plate.

Serving a plated and non-plated meal

The principal difference between serving a plated and a non-plated meal concerns the table place settings. When serving a plated meal, only charger plates are on the table, as the slave will be bringing food to the table already served on the dinner plate.

When serving individual dishes, the table is set (per the standing protocol) with the dinner plate placed on top of the charger plate. This arrangement includes the slave's place setting. In this situation, the slave has placed a second dinner plate in the kitchen, and after the slave has served Master (and other guests) the slave plates its meal in the kitchen. (This avoids any awkwardness at Table involved should the slave try to balance a tray of food in one hand and place food on its own dinner plate with its other hand.) As the slave finishes serving the last side dish to those seated at Table, it picks up the empty dinner plate (at its own place setting) and brings it to the kitchen. It immediately picks up the already-plated meal and returns immediately to Table where (walking counter-clockwise) it places the plate in front of its own chair.

At this point, the slave begins the wine service.

Serving protocols

Serving individual dishes is mechanically the same as serving a plated meal. The primary serving note is this: when the slave is offering a serving to someone, it must:

- Place the serving tray as close to the guest's dinner plate as possible so the person being served doesn't risk spilling food onto the table cloth;

- Stabilize the serving utensils to ensure that they don't fall off the serving tray onto the person's plate (or floor); and

- Rotate the serving tray in such a way that the person being served can easily pick them up in order to serve themselves.

The slave will serve Master first and from an Honor Present position (one knee on the floor). The order of remaining service is determined in advance according to the Order of Precedence for the evening, as Master has stipulated. The slave will bow at the waist when serving others.

Toasts

Once all food has been served, Master will nod to signal slave to offer our two toasts. Our personal toast is: "To our magical evenings and the days that support them." We touch glasses, take a sip of wine, and put the glasses back down on the table. slave next picks up and rings a small brass bell (obtained in Ballarat, Australia when he was there on a lecture tour in 2012) and says: "To our Leather Brethren everywhere." Again, we touch glasses, take a sip of wine, and put the glasses back down.

When dining with company, the slave will be attentive to any signal from Master that Master may wish to offer the toast that evening. If guests do not drink wine, slave will pour a fruit juice in their wine glass so they may toast with everyone else. When dining with company, our first toast is to welcome them to our home. (We generally do not speak our personal toast when others are present.)

Once all wine glasses are raised in the air, the person offering the toast will speak a few words. When glasses are raised for the toast, it is our protocol that Master's glass will always be the highest of the glasses coming together in this toast, and that the slave's glass will be the lowest. We don't make a fuss about this, as many dominant male guests are used to their glasses being the highest.

It is our house protocol that guests remain attentive during this stage and not offer a toast of their own unless they have asked to do so.

Dressing for the Evening

"Dressing" as a demarcation of intent

We use "dressing" for symbolic and psychological purposes. When you dress up, you feel special. When a man is in a tuxedo, he thinks of himself differently than when wearing shorts and drinking a beer with the neighbors. When a woman is wearing makeup suitable for a four-star restaurant, she turns heads. This change is important in a relationship, for it communicates to each person that the other will go the extra mile to look attractive. In this relationship, *clothing* communicates *caring*. This reasoning, this reality, underlies our choice to dress-to-impress and dine semi-formally in the evenings. It puts the spark in *sparkle*: it puts the magic in the magical world that we celebrate through words and deeds every evening.

Dressing for our evenings together isn't always tuxedos and floor-length gowns. Sometimes we dress for role-play. The slave may be a visiting Military attaché; I may be his date for the night. Or, I may be a slutty teenager and he's my Horrid Uncle who spanks me for no good reason at all. Sometimes, we just want to stream a movie and have a quiet evening: but we are still dressed in such a way that if someone rang our doorbell, they'd realize something different was going on here. We *never* (well, hardly ever) would appear to be "normally" dressed.[42]

Our attire sets the mood of the evening. The mood determines the evening's direction.

Levels of dress

Family events call for one of six levels of dress.

- Casual: Think "shopping at the mall." I prefer my slave to wear khakis (for men) rather than black jeans. Clothing should be starched and pressed.

- House uniform: The slave changes into its House Uniform upon arriving home from work but after it has performed any yard work or maintenance for which work clothes would be appropriate. The slave typically wears its House Uniform until about 7pm at which point we shower and changes into the clothing we'll wear for the evening.

- Fetish dress: This category includes any fetish clothing including military Mess Dress or tuxedo. Each relationship is different, and even within our relationship, our fetish outfits change over time, so no specifics can bo provided

- Formal: Black tuxedo jacket, white tie and tails, or white dinner jacket. If formal fetish, no shirt.

Master will indicate those occasions for which the slave will be gloved when serving. In a general way, the slave will provide gloved service for appetizers and again when serving the meal on those occasions when the slave is wearing Military Mess Dress, tuxedo or tails.

Pre-Dining Service

Serving cocktails

The slave will be gloved when serving drinks. Drinks will be placed on a serving tray when brought into a room.

Drinks will be arranged on the tray such that Master's drink is placed forward of all other drinks. Before drinks are offered to any guest, the slave will offer a drink to Master from a Full Present position (both knees on the ground). Drinks are then offered to guests from the tray.

Serving wine

Mentioned previously, it is important to give the wine bottle a rotating twist at the very end of the pouring cycle to ensure a dripless result. My slave will pour a small amount of wine into my glass. Master will sample the wine and signal whether to continue filling the glass or reject the bottle and open another. Once Master's glass has been filled, the slave will continue filling glasses according to the Order of Precedence.

Serving drinks and appetizers

Our usual protocol is to have drinks and appetizers in the living room while sitting on the couch. The slave first places foods on the coffee table and then returns to the kitchen to bring out Master's prepared drink, whether a cocktail or Port. The drink is served formally from a Full Present position.

If guests are present, the food service is the same, but the slave will present Master's drink first and then supply drinks according to the pre-determined Order of Precedence. In this case, the formality of the evening and the "protocol-awareness level" of guests determine how the slave serves Master's drink. If the guests are M/s, the slave will serve from Full Present. If the guests are BDSM, the slave will serve from Honor Present. If the guests are vanilla, the slave will remain standing when serving Master and offer a slight bow.

Dining Protocols

Notes about Table service

Service at a formal table will be efficient, quiet and unobtrusive. Nothing is ever taken directly from a slave's hands. Drinks are served on trays and food is served from a platter.

Formal plated service means that the slave will have put food on the dinner plate in the kitchen and brings it to the dining room and serves it to the guest from their left side, using its left hand.

When the slave places the initial plate in front of the guest, it is presented from the guest's left side using the slave's *left* hand (because of the angle of service). The plate rests in the palm of the slave's gloved hand and it uses its right hand to effect the plate's transfer from the left palm to the place setting. [Note: in traditional formal service, the dish or platter rests on a folded napkin placed on the flat of the servant's ungloved hand. We do NOT follow that protocol.]

Changing courses

The first course plate is removed from the guests' right side using slaves right hand. slave will secure utensils with the thumb of its right hand before lifting the plate. The second course, food already plated, is placed on the charger plate in the same manner as the first course.

Plated service, formal meal, two servers

To ensure gracefulness, our protocol for changing plates during a course change involves two steps rather than the traditional one step. First, the slave removes the used plate from the table, placing it on the empty portion of the tray held by it's assistant. Next, slave removes a fresh plate from the same tray and, placing it in the palm of its left hand, now places it before the guest.

Note #1: If my slave is serving alone, then we're back to the traditional single one-step process; all used plates will be removed before the second course is served.

Plated service, informal meal

Two dishes are removed at one time and two fresh dishes are brought to Table at one time.

Changing plates between courses, one server

The slave will walk counter-clockwise around the table. As it passes to Master's right, it will remove my used plate and take it to the kitchen. slave repeats this process as often as needed to clear the table. The slave will only remove one dish at a time and will not stack dishes. The slave will then bring one clean dish out at time and place it in front of each guest following the Order of Precedence chart. Master is always given the first clean plate.

Changing plates between courses, two servers

My slave's assistant will stand with a tray large enough to hold the plated next course plus sufficient room to place the used dish from the prior course. My slave (formally called the Table Server) will place a guest's used dish on the tray and then pick up a fresh dish from the tray and place it in front of the guest.

Dinner with guests

Starting time

Our dinners generally are served at eight o'clock, but Master will refine that time as situations dictate. Guests will have been informed that Harvey sounds the "Call to Table" by beginning to play the piano. Upon hearing Harvey, the slave will escort Master to Table.[43]

How to be seated

All dinner guests will be seated from the left side of the chair and will rise from their seats from the right side of the chair.

Who sits first?

The slave will seat Master, after which Master will signal other Dom/mess or Masters to seat their s-types or be seated, themselves, as their individual protocols dictate. My slave will remain standing until everyone is seated.

Serving a single guest or couple

Master will always be served before a guest unless the guest is a Leatherperson of senior rank.

If another Leatherslave is present and participating with us in a Leather scene involving an evening meal, then slave will remain responsible for ensuring Master's needs are met and the visiting Leatherslave will serve Master through this slave. This slave is not to serve the visiting Leatherslave.

Serving multiple couples
We will discuss serving procedures for larger groups in the next part of this Manual. See: "The process of serving food" in "Our Actual Dining Protocols."

What happens next?
Once Master has been seated, the slave will conduct our "*Centering Ritual.*" This takes place before serving the meal. This ritual evolved because slave wished a way to communicate to Master the special significance of being together. It is a form of mindfulness before sharing the meal.

The slave (who has remained standing) repositions itself behind Master's chair. It guides Master's head back so it is resting on the slave's chest. The slave strokes Master's forehead and runs its hands down Master's arms and over Master's breasts.[44]

At this point, the slave walks counter-clockwise around the table, and proceeds to serve the meal.

Once the meal has been served, the slave drops to Full Present position to Master's left and removes Master's napkin from the table. The slave unfolds the napkin one time (so the overall dinner napkin is folded in half) and after becoming focused, kisses the napkin and places it across Master's lap. If we are dining alone (or have pre-negotiated this bit with our guests), the slave then follows a protocol involving intimate touching. Master will release slave to continue with the wine service.

When dining with company, once the slave has placed Master's napkin (omitting the sexual touching part), Master will signal guests to place their own napkins.

If dining alone, slave now executes our private "wine-pouring protocol," explained in the "special table protocols" section, below.

Monitoring water and wine consumption
Liquids are traditionally served from the right side of the seated person, as the glasses are placed on the right side of the place setting. However, a left-handed guest may move their glass (or glasses) to the left side of the table setting for their own convenience. If so, the slave may refill their glasses from their left side to avoid reaching across them to pour wine. Some people may hold the glass up thinking it will help you to refill it. This action may cause a wine-pouring accident, so the slave must watch for this.

slave will closely monitor Master's water and wine glasses and will arise from Table and re-fill them, as needed. This is equally true when we have guests at Table. This is a form of anticipatory service, and it is to be accomplished without interrupting the conversation by asking whether Master (or any guest) wishes the glass refilled.

- <u>Water glass</u>: When refilling a water glass, pick up the glass and add the water/ice while the glass is positioned over the carpet to the right and slightly behind the guest.

- <u>Wine glass</u>: Wine glasses are refilled where they are sitting on the table. One does not pick up a wine glass to refill it.

Our Actual Dining Protocols

Preparing the house and table

Your house-prep checklist is attached in the supplementary material. In summary, here's what I expect to see before we start a formal evening together.

- slave is in its house uniform

- Wood floors are cleaned (preferably polished)

- Kitchen floor has been cleaned

- All kitchen counters are bare and freshly cleaned

- Outside lights are on and the front door is locked

- Flowers are decoratively displayed

- Table is fully set with the correct cutlery and stemware as appropriate to the dinner I've planned (or assigned you to prepare)

- All house lights are dimmed

- Fireplace is set either to burn logs or to display lit candles

- If Harvey is going to play for us, the slave will have prepared his music and pulled out the piano bench

- Thunderstorm CD is prepared on one sound system

- Any dinner music other than Harvey is selected and ready to play on the second sound system

- Living room is devoid of clutter; couch pillows are fluffed

Details relating to house maintenance

Whether in an apartment or a house, I require a fireplace in the living room. It's a threshold requirement. Wherever I live, the living room has to be large enough that I can place both the couch / coffee table AND the dining room table with equal view of the fireplace. This arrangement is fundamental to our chosen lifestyle.

When preparing the house, the slave will follow these guidelines:

- Living room: Furniture is correctly positioned. Items that normally belong on a table or shelf are in their proper places, the fireplace is pre-set either with wood or with candles, depending upon the season; every table lamp or oil lamp is either turned on or lit; additional candles are lit; all light-levels adjusted to an orange color-cast; all flower arrangements are correct and vases holding flowers are cleaned and filled with fresh water.

- <u>Kitchen</u>: all dishes have been cleaned and put away; counters are spotless and sanitized; floors have been swept and washed; sink is scoured; everything stored in its proper place.

- <u>Dining room</u>: centerpiece is correctly arranged and plate decorations are in place. If we are entertaining, place cards are out and name spellings have been verified with attending guests; condiments have been placed on the table. If this is a formal affair, dinner menus have been printed and placed on the dinner plate and a side table has been set up with the plate warmer.

Throughout the house, make a final check that all appears orderly and tidy. In bathrooms, verify the following:

- Waste paper baskets have been emptied and sanitized;

- Toilet bowls have been cleaned/sanitized;

- There is adequate toilet paper on the rolls and, if not, slave has changed the near-empty roll for a new roll and placed the expiring roll on top of the new one;

- In guest bathroom: verify that hand soap and hand towels are available and a box of facial tissue is on the counter.

Coming present before beginning our Evening

I distinguish between the slave being in the same room with me and it being "present" with me. I require emotional connection. Many of these protocols are designed with that intention.

From the time Master arrives home until we take our nighttime medications is reserved as our time to celebrate our relationship and to bond with one another. We fill this time with *ceremony*. There is a "greeting" ceremony when Master arrives home, then a cocktail ceremony after Master has attended to personal matters. I may want to spend an hour in the bath, so there is a bathing ceremony associated with that. And, if we're preparing dinner together, we have an elaborate dinner preparation ceremony.[45] Obviously, we also have a wide range of table-service protocols that we've just covered.

The slave will be dressed in its House Uniform when Master comes home. It will assume a Sanding Present or a Full Present position upon hearing the front door open (depending upon what it had been doing when Master arrived, thus how fast it can take a formal position). The slave will remove any encumbering items from Master's hands. Master will generally give slave a light kiss or recognition. Master takes about fifteen minutes attending to personal needs.

Having changed clothes, Master returns to the living room. Most commonly, the slave has set out cheeses and crackers and either a cocktail (Cosmo or Bloody Mary) or a glass of Port for Master and Manhattan or Port for slave. We use this time to debrief about each of our days.

At this time my preferred cocktail recipes follow:

Cosmo by Anya (Capri Hotel Bar, Augusta, GA)

- 1½ shot SKKY Vodka
- ½ shot triple sec
- 1 splash Rose's lime juice
- 2 oz. cranberry juice

Bloody Mary

- 1½ oz. vodka
- 3 oz. tomato juice
- 1 oz. lemon juice
- ½ teaspoon Worcestershire sauce
- 3 drops Tabasco sauce
- Pepper
- Salt
- ¼ teaspoon celery salt
- ½ tablespoon prepared horseradish

While this section describes the majority of our early-evening protocols that lead to sexual play, there are times when Master wishes the evening to be used differently. A "different" evening may involve:

- Exercising,
- Having an early dinner so we can go dancing,
- Reading or writing for 60-90 minutes,
- Streaming a movie,
- Etc.

Sometimes we lose track of time. To safeguard against losing the evening to minutiae (or work), 7pm is designated as a time to come present and reevaluate what we are doing. The protocol to cover this "coming aware of the evening" calls for the slave to keep track of the time and to alert me as it's getting close to 7. The specific wording is: "Master, with respect, this slave points out that it is nearly 7 o'clock. Does Master have any special preferences for dinner or for how the balance of the evening will go?" (Obviously, this sentence is subject to reasonable modifications: I may already have told the slave what I want for dinner; I may already have indicated my choice for after-dinner activities, etc.)

At any rate, this is the time I tell the slave about the intent of the evening and whether that requires special dress or specific activities.[46] We now shower and change clothes. If it is a Monday, Wednesday, or Friday, the slave will trim its beard and perform other body cleansing/shaving protocols as previously described (see: "health and hygiene").

Some special table protocols
Pouring wine
slave will then place my napkin on my lap as per protocol. While the general napkin-placing protocol has already been described, we have a private protocol at this point. After placing the folded napkin in my lap (and before rising), the slave will check that all is "in order" with my genitals. Once assured that everything is where it should be and is appropriately moist, the slave rises and walks around the table to pick up the wine bottle. If red wine, it is in a wine caddy; if white wine, it is in a chiller.

Now carrying the wine bottle, the slave continues walking counterclockwise around the table. As it passes behind my chair, slave will pull down its pants in order that its genitals are exposed by the time it pivots left and is standing (squarely) to my right. From this position, two things happen: first, the slave will pour my wine; second, I will fondle its privates (or more). This continues until I hear that the wine is no longer being poured: slave is encouraged to pour the wine slowly.

When our wine glasses are full, slave will continue on its path around the table, replacing the wine in the wine caddy or chiller and taking its own seat.

Offering toasts

As previously detailed, we offer two toasts before beginning the meal. It is my preference that my slave offers these two toasts.

The slave now takes an "attending" position while seated: hands in lap. It will not eat until I've fed it a taste from my plate. There is a reason I feed the first bite of food to my slave: the slave is my official food tester. I require it to take the first bite to ensure that it hasn't tried to poison me with its cooking. It has sometimes occurred that the expression on slave's face cautions me about the size of bite that I next take. We have had three instances over our five years together when we deemed the meal inedible.

The slave will follow this protocol when we are dining out.

Master enjoys being fed by the slave and may request this after feeding slave the first bite.

Picking up food

It is our House Protocol that we do not use our fingers to pick up food. These are the only acceptable exceptions:

- Moving pieces of bread to your mouth from the bread plate

- We have served a delicacy that is impossible to eat with a fork or spoon (such as hors d'oeuvres, canapés, crudités)

- Artichoke

- Chips, French fries, and hamburgers. You may use two fingers to stabilize fried chicken as you use a knife or fork to remove the meat from the bone. Both hands may not be sullied.

- Cookies (breaking off a bite sized piece—avoid bringing the entire cookie to your mouth)

- Crisp bacon (but not limp bacon)

- Olives, celery and pickles

- Sandwiches that are not open-faced, not too tall to fit in the mouth, not saturated with dripping sauces or loaded with mushy fillings. That is, sandwiches that are intended to be picked up and eaten—otherwise use your fork and knife

- Small fruits and berries on the stem, most often, fresh strawberries with the hulls attached

If we do have to use our fingers, slave will have anticipated this before dinner and will have prepared finger bowls for use and the correct colored napkin.

Dinner Ending Protocols

Finishing a meal

The slave will take extreme care not to end its meal before Master. If slave is entertaining Master during dinner (thus may not be eating) Master will consider that when pacing the meal.

Master will signal dinner's end. Upon getting the signal, the slave will ask: "Is Master ready to be cleared from Table?"[47]

The slave will assist Master from table before removing the remnants of the dinner. There may be times when Master directs the slave to clear the used dishes as we remain at table for conversation or ambiance. The slave will do this as unobtrusively as possible.

Table-clearing and cleanup protocols

Generally, Master wishes the slave to join in conversation after dinner. Sometimes Master will permit the slave to clear the table and soak the dishes; other times not. If we have planned a sexual evening, Master wishes to flow from the table to the living room without clearing Table. (99% of our sexual activity is in the living room.)

If nothing particular was planned after dinner, the slave will clear and soak the dishes and generally clean up in the kitchen. As that process takes about 30 minutes, the slave will rejoin Master in the living room for the balance of the evening.

As we are going to bed, the slave will have approximately 30 minutes to finish hand-washing dishes. Under no circumstances will the slave put silver, stemware, or china in the dishwasher. The dishwasher is to be used as a drying rack.

The slave is to keep track of this 30 minutes and will stop and join Master in bed once the time is up. The slave is not to get distracted and continue cleaning beyond this point.

The slave will handle any remaining cleanup before work in the morning, including using the Hoover Floor Mate to wash the floor.

Resetting the table
The slave will fully reset the table before determining that it has completed the kitchen cleanup procedures. As previously described, "resetting the table" means hand drying and polishing all china, stemware, and cutlery. As needed, the slave will give the silver a light touch-up with the silver-polishing cloth.

128

Section Three Footnotes
Footnotes 38-47

38   In designing the Order of Precedence chart, there are at least two possibilities:

   • To seat the next highest ranking person to the right of the highest ranking person, and the third highest ranking person right of the second highest, etc., and continue until the person of lowest rank sits left of the highest ranking person, or

   • To begin with the second highest ranking person to the right of the highest ranking person, then put the third highest ranking person to the left of the highest ranking person, and continue alternating to the left and right until the lowest ranking person is positioned furthest from the highest ranking.

   Master will determine the seating pattern and provide the slave with the typed list.

39   An Internet search will produce sites that will give you suggestions about selecting wines as a function of the food being served. From there, you can derive the type of wine glasses that will be set out.

40   As you can probably anticipate from the details you've already read, we care about the temperature at which our wines are served. If you're going to all the trouble to create a spectacular dinner event, you're going to want to attend to such details as the wine's

temperature. Success at this level of detail affects the overall success of the dinner's presentation. The relevant adage—first recorded in 1788—is "a miss is as good as a mile." So: here you go...

Wine service is as much art as science. In a general sense, white wines are chilled and can be opened at the last minute. Here are the official serving temperatures for whites:

- "Young" whites   50–53 degrees
- "Mature" whites   53–57 degrees

Rosés are supposed to be served at temperatures ranging between 53 to 57 degrees.

Reds are another matter. There are two dynamics working with red wines. The first involves aerating them; the second involves chilling them.

Red wines should be opened about 30 minutes before you're intending to pour them so it can "breathe." The concept, here, is to expose the wine to the surrounding air to warm up to "open up" the wine's aromas. You're doing this in order to improve the wine's overall flavor characteristics. Of course, this process probably has more meaning to someone who can distinguish a $150 bottle of wine from a $15 bottle of wine. Personally, we can't. However, we dutifully open bottles of red wine about half an hour before pouring them.

Now: unlike people of a certain class in centuries past who actually *had* wine cellars, people today generally serve red wines that are kept in the house. Since your home's temperature is in the 70-75 degree range, that's also the probable temperature of your red wine. However, that temperature conflicts with professional advice about the optimal pouring temperatures of reds. Enologists instruct that red wines should be offered at the following temperatures:

- "New" reds   50–57 degrees
- "Mature" reds   61–65 degrees
- Sparkling wines   50–53 degrees
- Sweet wines   50–65 degrees

Unless you're storing your wines in a refrigerator designed to maintain that temperature, your only reliable option is to purchase a wine chiller/warmer that will cool/heat one or two bottles at a time. Unfortunately, there are not many choices along these lines: I'll leave the research to you.

41   The practice of walking counter-clockwise around the table had sexual origins. Bob would require his slave to walk "sexily" around the table and when she was pouring wine he would play with her genitals.

As we have now explained in the text, when the slave is pouring wine for me, our protocol calls for him to have his genitals out and available for me to play with when he assumes the "wine pouring" position.

I will fondle (or more) until I hear that he has finished pouring the wine.

42   Actually, one of our most active fantasies is that somebody—anybody—will ring our doorbell at about 9pm some night and join us. It's never happened, unfortunately.

43   If you have not seen the motion picture "Harvey," this is not going to make much sense. To remind you, Harvey (the original movie was released in 1950 and the excellent remake came out in 1996) is an invisible rabbit. (Actually, Harvey is a Pooka, a shape-changing spirit of Irish lore that can bring both good and bad fortune.)

When you first enter our home, Harvey (a 5'7" rabbit dressed in a grey Morning Suit and top hat), is there to greet you. Eccentrics that we are, we have a Yamaha acoustic piano (the Disclavier model) that can be played either by hand or by computer. The external control panel controls its volume. Harvey can be set to play quietly while we're entertaining or at dinner.

Part of slave's pre-Evening prep involves turning on the Yamaha's computer, inserting the correct disk to match our mood, and hit the "play" and then "pause" buttons so it's ready to play as our signal that it's time to move from the living room to take our seats at Table.

Out of courtesy to the spirit of Harvey, we always pull out the piano seat before he arrives, and speak with him as though he is our piano player for the evening. Per our "contract," we always make sure that he takes his union breaks after playing for us for about 45 minutes.

44   This is a time when sexual touching is introduced into our dinner service. The slave will fondle various parts of Master's arms/torso (including breasts), as part of this ceremony.

45   One of our favorite "play toys" is a 10" butcher knife. We often play sexually when preparing dinner together, particularly if it is a Dining In evening (seriously dressy). There are various "playing-in-the-kitchen protocols." My favorite kitchen protocol is the "Master is bending over" rule. If Master bends over (she bends from her waist and doesn't wear underwear) that means this slave is to fondle her genitals and/or spank her. Fingering often leads to squirting. Also, the big butcher knife makes a nice stingy paddle when the blade is smacked against her and when reversed, the handle provides a great thuddy implement. I don't need to describe the "normal" play aspects of a 10" butcher knife to those reading this book. Let's just say: I recommend 10" butcher knives. Expensive knives tend to be heavier. Heavier is better.

46   We have found it very helpful to discuss early in the evening the intent of that evening. We found that when we didn't do that, the evenings drifted without purpose. Also, Master prefers to prepare psychologically if we're going to have a sexual evening.

Further, we decide well ahead of time whether the sm play will be sensual or heavy.

47   This is a little inside joke. When dinner ends, Master wishes the conversation to shift to the living room. Master does not wish to interrupt the flow with the slave clearing off the dinner dishes. So: we clear Master rather than clearing the table.

Section Four
Specialized Services

Figuring out what to do with Bob as my slave was something of a challenge. Not only is he highly educated, but he's also had an extremely broad range of life-experiences.

- Graduated high school from The International School of Geneva, Switzerland (1962)

- Spent a summer teaching English in the Jewish ghetto of Tehran, Iran, then continued around the world for a month visiting exotic cities. (1965)

- BA in Education with secondary school teaching certificate. (1966)

- Taught high school English for three years in Los Angeles' inner city.

- Awarded Ford Foundation Fellowship to begin his doctoral studies at the University of Wisconsin. (1970)

- With his future wife, walked the full 220 miles of the John Muir Trail carrying their entire three weeks food supply. (1971)

- Awarded a Visiting Fellowship grant by the National Institute of Justice (the research branch of the U.S. Department of Justice) to study and write about crime in public schools. (1976)

- Wrote the very first doctoral dissertation on crime in public schools. Awarded PhD, University of Wisconsin. (1977)

- The original incorporator of the American Association of Woodturners. Developed and was Managing Editor of their quarterly publication. (1986)

- Co-founded and for 14 years ran the non-profit National Alliance for Safe Schools. Developed and was Managing Editor of their quarterly publication. (1977-1992)

- After 9 years as a commodity and stock trader, joined a boutique Washington, DC stock and commodity futures brokerage firm. Was made a principal of the commodities firm within the first year, became a VP a year later, and after another year, was asked to be firm's president. (1992-1996)

- Yes, the next 20 years remained as intense but the focus shifted to reading, writing, and lecturing about BDSM and Master/slave topics.

Thinking it would be "helpful," he gave me his professional resume early in our relationship. Without his publications list, it comes to 11 pages and 3,800 words. Then there are the four pages of publications. Truly, it was stunning.

I could go on, but you get the idea. I'd never met anyone faintly like him. We had differing backgrounds but (fortunately) some common similarities. Remember: the slave is 20 years older than I am.

Back to the opening sentence: it took me a while to figure out what in the world I was going to do with him as my slave. Ultimately, I broke his functions down into groups. Those are listed in this part of the protocol manual.

Personal Assistant

Here's a quote from your former mentor, Officer Wes of San Diego. I can't think of a better way to start this part of your Manual.

> It's My personal belief that once My slave enters into service to Me, everything it does is some form of service to Me. Breathing is a form of service. Striving to spread a smile at work is a form of service. Maintaining the slave quarters is a form of service. All the chopping-wood/carrying-water of life is a form of service. The idea here is to encourage My slave to view EVERYTHING as an opportunity to be of service to Me; thereby manifesting deeper connection to all of humanity/the universe.
>
> 2006, private letter

Maintain "The Book of Master"

The slave will create and continually update "The Book of Master." This book will detail my personal preferences, needs, and wants

Basic relationship rules (see supplemental material)

Master's values

Things that trigger Master

Vital notes about Master

Good things to do now

In her own words, Master is...

Critical needs

Important health notes

Master's LIKES

Gift ideas for Master

Things Master does NOT like

Foods that are not good for Master

How to make... (drinks, special meals, etc.)

Vacation ideas

"Surprise Trip" Workaround (Master does not like surprises.)

Miscellaneous notes

Master Says...

Key protocols/behaviors

Flirtations and sex

Evening requirements

Notes for men who will have sex with Master

Master's size and measurements

Notes about SM play

Notes about sex-play

Psychological test results

Social secretary

My slave maintains my social calendar. It is also expected to be my point-of-contact for most people, even some of my friends. I don't like speaking on the phone or doing email as I am doing that all day as part of my job.

My slave is responsible for keeping me up-to-date with news/information within our Community.

Keeping track of events and guests

The slave will use two sets of logs to keep track of what we serve our guests and their preferences. One log records our events/dinners and includes the guest list. The other log details our guests' preferences and specifics of the event.

The slave will record gifts brought by guests; slave is responsible for preparing written thank-you notes for Master to send. The logs are included in the supplementary material.

Arranging for entertainment

Master enjoys dressing up and being taken out to diner. In such cases, Master may or may not name a particular restaurant. If not, Master may explain the type of food, level of service, and price range. My slave is responsible for conducting necessary Internet research to determine two (and only two) options. When presenting the options, slave will provide the reasons for recommending these two restaurants.

At times, Master simply requests to be taken to dinner and lets the slave exercise discretion in making plans and suggest the preferred level of dress. While it is rare that Master will change clothes and makeup for the slave, it happens from time to time.

The slave should prompt Master for entertainment preferences for the weekend by the prior Wednesday. This could include theater, cinema, music, or dance. The slave will conduct an Internet research and inform Master of a few options. Upon direction, the slave will make necessary reservations and purchase tickets.

We generally do not invite individuals or couples over at the last minute.

Travel management

When Master wants to travel somewhere, slave will handle logistics including interesting places to go, associated costs, and comments.

Once the trip has been identified, the slave will create a travel folder to contain everything we need. The slave will begin to fill in the pre-trip checklist (provided in the Supplements) and staple it to the front of the trip folder. The slave is responsible for:

- Managing all negotiations for the trip.

- Arranging for flight and hotel reservations, including linking our hotel or airline reward numbers with these reservations.

- Providing an itinerary that specifies when we are leaving the house on the outbound leg and landing on the return leg.

- Obtaining adequate cash for the trip.

- Providing (a day before departure) detailed weather report covering our travel period.

On-site Logistics: Concurrent with making hotel reservation, slave will speak with the hotel's concierge desk and identify names and locations of any "don't miss" places in the city. it will also determine the names and websites for any particularly romantic restaurants. Master likes really interesting places. High visual. Interesting foods.

Driving and Car Maintenance

My slave has no standing responsibilities concerning my car. When I want something done, I will let you know.

The slave will keep its car neat on the inside, the floors vacuumed: I don't like to see clutter when being driven around town. I expect slave to have its own car's oil changed every 3,500 miles and the tires rotated every 10,000 miles. The slave is to devise a way of keeping track of this.

I would prefer that you keep your car reasonably washed. I don't want you to let it get to the point that I have to say something.

slave will serve as Master's chauffeur when we go out. In that role, the slave will drive very conservatively and drive slightly under the posted speed limits. Master does not like to be frightened by anyone's driving habits. The slave will take particular care to slow down well in advance of stopped traffic or a red light. Master does not like rapid braking.

The slave's car is always to have adequate fuel to be able to go out in an evening.

Safety and security issues
Lost wallet or purse
Basic ID security protocols:

- No credit card is signed with our names. The phrase "Ask for ID" will be written in the signature space.

- The slave is to maintain photocopies of both sides of all documents and credit cards we carry in our purse/wallet The backsides of the credit cards contain the credit card names, numbers, and customer support phone numbers to contact to notify of the loss.

- These papers are to be kept in folder along with our House Manual.

The slave is to update this log quarterly.
Protocols if we've only lost a wallet containing drivers' license and credit cards.

- After doing the obvious (retracing steps, calling places we may have left it, etc.) the cardholder will begin calling card companies and notifying them of the loss.

- We will next notify the three credit reporting agencies of the lost cards. (Equifax, Experian, and Trans Union)

- If we suspect theft rather than accidental loss, we will file a police report and notify the Social Security Administration's fraud line: 800-269-0271.

Illness

Illness of either person brings up protocol and role-image issues.

It can be VERY hard on an incapacitated slave to accept service from its Master. It is very disorienting for Master to be serving slave; it affects a slave's sense-of-self.

In this relationship, "Master being ill" is covered under "Rule 2." The slave has specific authority to take over relationship leadership to the extent necessary to preserve our union. We have no protocols for Master, of course.

Determine what personality level is expected of Master when slave is ill and also what personality level is expected of slave when master is ill. The issue: being upset that master is taking care of slave.

The slave will keep a list of all my medical professionals and their phone numbers. This list, and one for itself, will be kept in physical form in the kitchen pantry in our ICE book. (In Case of Emergency). The names, addresses, and phone numbers of all relevant hospitals and emergency clinics will be included in that book.

It is VERY important for people in nontraditional relation-ships to draw up certain documents.

- Living wills,
- Advance healthcare directives,
- Wills,
- Durable powers of attorney, and
- Spousal agreements.

Legal documents

This section concerns wills, advance directives, and pow-ers of attorney.

I've heard a number of horror-stories concerning M/s cou-ples who have run into problems with relatives or medical personnel when one person becomes ill or dies. To prevent that, my slave is to be familiar with actions we both will take to protect one another in such situations.

Wills, advanced directives, and financial powers of attorney are part of Master's ethical responsibility to the slave. In our case, I have endeavored to structure ours to replace the rights of a spouse to access their partner's medical re-cords. We both have structured our wills to clarify rights of survivorship that are taken for granted by married couples. Here is a quick overview of the legal items that we had to learn about and create.

Will

A will (that has been filed with your county and whose exis-tence is known by close friends or select family members) is a legal document that specifies how your property and assets should be distributed after death. (Unless you have substantial wealth, it's very easy to use an online legal services company to create a will that will be recognized in your State of residence.)

The tricky part about the will concerned our property distribution list. I am still married and have two grown/married children. My husband declines to prepare a will. I am estranged from all of them. Nonetheless, my will states my current wishes regarding specific items. You are responsible for ensuring all my legal documents (and yours, also) are kept where I can easily find them. You will keep that location listed on your computer in the file named: "_ If I am injured or die" immediately within your "My Documents" folder. (Note: by starting the file with an underscore, you force it to the top of all other files or folders.)

Living will (advance healthcare directives)

A living will refers to a set of healthcare directives (in the form of Powers of Attorney) that tell your medical professionals how you want specific situations dealt handled. In addition to our wills, we will each maintain and annually review *advance healthcare directives*. These contain instructions for medical treatments if either of us becomes incapacitated.

There are some subtle areas that concern advance healthcare directives. The specific way my slave and I addressed these are private, but since we're publishing this Protocol Manual, I'll provide the list of topics we had to decide upon. Hint: you're probably going to want to consult an ER nurse or your own physician about what you should/should not (can/can not) specify in your State. Medicine is changing so dramatically that you need to consult a professional before finalizing these.)

- Resuscitation: Resuscitation restarts the heart when it has stopped beating. You will have to decide if (and when) you would want to be resuscitated by cardiopulmonary resuscitation (CPR) or by a device that delivers an electric shock to stimulate the heart. If you do not want anyone to try to resuscitate you, you'll need to have a valid "DNR" on file with the doctor, the hospital, and your attorney.

- "No heroic measures:" Medication is not considered "heroic". Resuscitation is considered to be an "heroic measure." But, under some circumstances, other treatments may be considered heroic as well. These can include mechanical ventilation, feeding tubes, etc. Try to be as specific as you can about the kinds of treatments you would want under different circumstances.

- Mechanical ventilation: Mechanical ventilation takes over your breathing if you're unable to do so. Consider if, when and for how long you would want to be placed on a mechanical ventilator.

- Tube feeding: Tube feeding supplies nutrients and fluids intravenously or through a tube in the stomach. Decide if, when, and for how long you would want to be fed in this manner.

- <u>Dialysis</u>: Dialysis removes waste from your blood and manages fluid levels if your kidneys no longer function. Determine if, when and for how long you would want to receive this treatment.

- <u>Antibiotics or antiviral medications</u>: These medications are used to treat many infections. If you were near the end of life, would you want infections to be treated aggressively or would you rather let infections run their course? Remember: you can be near the end of your life well before "old age."

- <u>Comfort care (palliative care)</u>: This includes any number of interventions that may be used to keep you comfortable and manage pain while also following your other treatment wishes. This may include being allowed to die at home, getting pain medications, being fed ice chips to soothe dryness, and avoiding invasive tests or treatments.

- <u>Organ and tissue donations</u>: If your organs are to be removed for donation, you will be kept on life-sustaining treatment temporarily—until the procedure is complete. To help medical professionals avoid any confusion, you'll want to state in your living will that you understand the need for this temporary intervention.

- <u>Donating your body:</u> If you're considering donating your body to science, you'll need to contact a local medical school, university, or donation program for information on how to register for a planned donation for research.

The slave will also maintain a separate, limited medical POA for each of us. This POA gives us hospital visiting rights plus access to one another's medical records.

Financial POAs

The slave is also responsible for maintaining our Financial Powers of Attorney (POAs). We have two of them:

- Limited financial POA: We each are to have access to one another's checking accounts in the event of either of us being incapacitated. These are to be "springing" POAs, effective only upon the signature of a physician that one of us is unable to attend to our financial responsibilities for more than a month.

- Durable financial POA: Again, this is a "springing" POA, effective upon a physician's signature that one of us is either going to be incapacitated for more than six months or is dead. This gives full powers to the other to manage all financial matters. Period. Wording in our wills backs it up.

Valet Services

Personal care of Master

Bedtime

The slave has two bedtime protocols. The first is to turn down the comforter and sheets on Master's side of the bed; second is to ensure Master has taken appropriate evening medications.

slave will turn off the overhead light, turn off the bureau lamp, plug in its phone and set weekday alarms in order to get up in the morning to make Master's tea.

Grocery shopping

The slave is responsible not only for keeping the shopping list updated, but also for doing the grocery shopping. The slave is responsible for ensuring that we do not run out of any of standard items (eggs, milk, cheeses, etc.) The slave is also responsible for preparing most dinners.

When the last of any item in the pantry is opened, it must be listed on the current shopping list.

- Meats: slave will take care to purchase high-quality meats, attending to the grade of the meat (prime beef preferred) and the amount of marbling.

- Fruits and vegetables: Master prefers that certain items *always* to be available in the house. This includes: Honeycrisp apples, avocados, red and white onions, bacon, eggs, smoked almonds, cheeses, Truscuit, etc.

- The secondary list to be kept in supply includes: black seedless grapes, bananas, salad fixings, milk, applesauce, cottage cheese, etc.

- Items such as asparagus, parsley, and celery will be stored in water in the refrigerator.

Shoe and boot care

I like my slave to look sharp: that includes nicely shined shoes and boots. The slave is responsible for establishing and maintaining a nice polish on both of our shoes and boots.

Supply list:

- Tin of Kiwi black "Parade Gloss" shoe polish
- Large Kiwi 100% horsehair shine brush)
- Kiwi shoe polish applicator brush
- Cotton balls
- Professional shoe shine buffing cloth

The slave is to spread supplies and shoes on the bath towel designated as the "shoe shine towel."
Clean the shoes. Remove dust and dirt with the horsehair shine brush or damp rag. If they get a little wet, allow them time to dry before applying the polish.

Using the applicator brush, liberally cover the shoe or boot. The goal is a thin coat of polish that is evenly applied. Pay particular attention to the seams of the shoe. Allow the polish to dry for 15 minutes, minimum.

Use the horsehair shine brush to brush the entire shoe vigorously. The slave is doing this in order to brush off the excess polish. The goal is to leave only a small film of polish on the outside of the shoe.

Once the entire shoe has been covered and brushed, it is time to put a mirror shine on the toe. Dip a cotton ball or pad into some water and squeeze out the excess moisture so the cotton ball is merely damp, not dripping. Put a little polish on the damp cotton. With small circular motions, apply the polish on the toe.

Repeat this last step until the toe has a mirror surface. Use a new piece of cotton each time the dab of polish has been used up. All excess polish must have been removed before applying a new coating.

The initial shine is the hardest: it will become easier each time you do it. Expect to spend about 45 minutes the first time you establish a shine, and about 20 minutes per shine on an ongoing basis.

Housecleaning

The slave is responsible for the cleanliness of the house.

Daily Housekeeping

Ensure all surfaces are neat and tidy, nothing out of place.

In the Master bath:

- Ensure clean towels are tri-folded and hung evenly;

- Ensure the toilet is clean;

- Polish chrome water faucets on the vanity, in the bath, and in the shower;

- Wipe counter surfaces with disinfectant. Nothing shall be left on the counters;

- Attend to the mirror, as needed;

- Empty trash can;

- Keep toilet paper stocked in the TP dispenser;

- Attend to status of grout in shower.

Attend to other rooms in the house, as needed (little, if anything, should be needed).

- Living room: put everything away and re-place couch pillows (after fluffing them).

- Front bathroom: empty trash (if needed); keep toilet paper

In the kitchen:

- Dishes: Hand wash everything; do not use dishwasher—too harsh on the china and silver and use a dishcloth and not a scrubber or sponge. The slave misses lip marks on glass rims when not using a dishcloth. Use the dishwasher as a drying rack for plates. Use Dawn® kitchen soap. Use rubber gloves.

- Stemware: Hand wash using lukewarm water; rinse well under running water. To obtain extra sparkle, hold the glasses over some steaming water for 30 seconds. Use a lint-free linen towel without any fabric softener to dry stem and glassware. Hold the glass by the bowl, not the stem, which is fragile, and gently polish off the water. Don't force the towel into the bowl as the glass is thin and might break.

Just leave the glass turned upside down and let it drain itself onto a towel before final touching-up with the linen towel.

- Counter surfaces: Scour the kitchen sink and related counters. Use Cameo® to scour a stainless steel kitchen sink; use Barkeeper's Friend® for a porcelain sink. Also use Barkeeper's Friend® to clean all kitchen counter surfaces. Use 409® to clean the stovetop and stove vent. Use a paper towel to dry the sink and counters after cleaning.

- Refrigerator: Label and date all leftovers put into the refrigerator. Use plastic storage containers or Vaccuseal® containers for leftovers. I do not like amorphous plastic bags put into the refrigerator. Keep refrigerator shelves orderly and clean spills when they occur. I don't want to have to ask you to clean the refrigerator or freezer.

- Pantry: Keep the pantry floor clean and tidy. It is not to be used as a collection ground for items that will not fit on a shelf.

- Kitchen floor: Maintain the floor. At least three times a week, either before bed or before leaving for work in the morning, use the electric floor-cleaning machine to wash the floor.

- Dining room table: Fully reset the dining room table before bed at night or before leaving for work in the morning.

Weekly housecleaning

Use a spray kitchen cleanser on the stove's surface, vent area, and back-splash. Use Bartenders Friend®, not Ajax® on Formica surfaces and in kitchen and bathroom sinks. Clean the bathtub and shower with soap scum removing cleanser; use a grout/tile-specific cleaner in the shower, as needed.

Additionally:

- Remove and shake out kitchen rugs.

- Use the electric hard-floor cleaning machine to clean the kitchen floor.

- On applicable floors, apply wood-floor cleaner/polish.

- Clean the bathroom mirrors.

- Vacuum the remainder of the house.

- Do a "light dusting" throughout the house including the pianos.

- Check all walls and molding around light switches and door handles for smudge marks; remove same.

Depending upon the season, either clean ashes out of fireplace and sweep the hearth, or clean up and dripped wax in the fireplace and replace candles, as needed. Seasonally, the slave is responsible for purchasing firewood and ensuring an adequate is on the clean hearth.

Monthly housecleaning

Monthly, the slave will do a "heavy dusting." That means books and art objects. It also means polishing the pianos and cleaning the windowsills. Apply leather conditioner to leather-covered furniture.

Remove everything from refrigerator and clean all surfaces. Clean top of refrigerator, washer and dryer; clean inside surfaces for both the microwave and the oven.

If we are living in a house or apartment that uses electric burners with "overflow protectors," lift out and clean all stove burners; lift the entire stove surface and clean below the elements. As necessary, replace the aluminum "spill protectors" that fit immediately below the heating elements.

Run an empty load through the dishwasher and ensure that it is spotless, inside and out. (Note to readers: we don't normally use our dishwasher. Everything is hand-washed.)

Check AC filters: and change as necessary.

Quarterly housecleaning

Clean all baseboards and woodwork. Clean all windows, inside and outside if possible. Clean all ceiling fan blades. Clean the freezer.

Once a quarter, the slave is to clean every drawer in the kitchen and master bathroom. This means:

- Remove contents from drawer
- Take drawer out of it's drawer-slide
- Totally clean or replace drawer liners
- Replace contents
- Reorganize the drawer to be visually attractive

Yard care

The slave is expected to be competent at yard work. This includes lawn mowing and lawn edging, trimming bushes, pruning trees, and so forth.

The slave will know how to take care of yard maintenance equipment including fueling, sharpening, storing, and handling lawn mowers, trimmers, weed-eaters, and the like. If the slave deems a repair is beyond its repair skill level, it is responsible for finding a competent repair shop.

The slave will mow the lawn approximately every five days during the height of the growing season and as-needed at other times. The slave will also check plants to be sure they have been adequately watered. slave needs to monitor and manage the potted plants, whether in the afternoon before Master arrives or in the morning before it leaves for work.

As needed, the slave will use the forced-air blower to keep walkways and back porch clear from debris.

Chef services

The slave is expected to master a variety of meals to add variety to Masters life. This includes breakfasts, lunches, dinners, and appetizers.

The slave will become particularly adept at the art of pre-senting food on a plate and setting an attractive Table. Art matters in all its forms.

Knife maintenance
Master recognizes that the slave is passionate about its carbon steel (as opposed to stainless steel) kitchen knives and brought its own set of Wüsthof knives with him. slave has developed its own protocols concerning them.

- Using the Wüsthof sharpening steel, put a fine edge on the knife before each use.

- Hand wash, dry, and put away all kitchen knives.

- After using the Dexter Russell 10" wood-handled chef's knife, immediately wash it and dry it, partic-ularly the handle. (Apply mineral oil to the handle, as needed.)

Food presentation
The slave will maintain a supply of items to add color to our plates:

- Candied apples
- Curly parsley
- Small carrots
- Spiced peaches
- Etc.

Serving Condiments
This is a list of condiments we commonly serve with certain foods. These must always be kept in stock:

- Apple sauce
  - With some pork dishes
  - Every time potato pancakes are served (pot roast and...)
  - As a side for lunches
- Cranberry sauce
  - Chicken
  - Turkey
- Mint jelly
  - Lamb

Portions

The slave is to prepare only portions for the number of people dining. Pre-measure the portions to match our dining habits. For example, if each person typically consumes five spears of asparagus, only cook 10 spears. If each person typically consumes $1/4$ cup of snap beans, only prepare $1/2$ cup. The goal is not to have any leftovers that then must be refrigerated.

Storing and Packaging Foods

At the slave's discretion, leftovers will be wrapped in plastic wrap, placed in plastic storage containers, or vacuum-sealed.

At no time is a "take-home" box to be placed in the refrigerator; the food that has been brought home is to be individually wrapped and stored or vacuusealed. Foods are to be labeled with packaging date and contents.

Miscellaneous Service Protocols

"Sparkly service"

The difference between "A" service and "A+" service lies both in the pre-planning and in the attention to details. I've included an article on anticipatory service in the supplementary materials. I asked the slave to list some examples of this in our relationship: this is that list.

Relating to food, prep, or the Table:

- Rather than using cane sugar, we use "decorative sparkling sugar."

- As we use powdered sugar on our waffles, pancakes and French Toast, we have an antique powdered sugar dispenser.

- We use "silence pads" in the sink and counter to lower kitchen sounds when cleaning up.

- The slave uses SOS to scrub the bottoms of pots after every use so they continue to look attractive.

- The slave makes "stuff" go away from the dinner table without any visible fuss. As the dinner proceeds, unneeded plates/glasses/cutlery just seem to go away.

- When Dining Out, the slave polishes Master's cutlery before placing them in their correct position on the table.

Communicating "I love you":

- Texting a few times throughout the workday to maintain connection.

- Occasionally putting love notes in Master's lunch box or on Master's pillow or dinner plate.

- Both of our dinner plates have romantic things on them. On Master's plate: a love-note card, a leather rose, and a little red glass heart. On the slave's plate, a pair of wire-rimmed glasses and a black bow tie.

- Always opening Master's car door when she is getting into or out of a car.

- Nightly, turning down the corner of Master's bed.

- Serving nightly medications in Full Present: same protocol for serving a cocktail.

- In the winter, starting her car and turning on the heater 15 minutes before she has to leave.

Relating to the house or yard:

- Use two independent sound systems in the living room: one plays a thunderstorm, the other plays our music selection for the evening.

- Strobe lights flash when triggered by the thunder

- Holiday lights on a remote "on/off" switch brighten up the back yard in the evenings. Some are woven around tree trunks, others are in bushes.

- Dimmers are installed for all light switches throughout the house. This produces a warm feel in the evenings.

- Always rent apartments/homes with a wood-burning fireplace.

- Ensure toilet paper storage containers remain filled.

- Ensure toilet paper lies over the top of the roll rather than falls behind the roll.

Sex

slave's sexual arts

I have always appreciated your sexual prowess. Your wide knowledge of the art of sexual connection makes our evenings memorable. The slave is to continue to learn, practice, and explore in all areas related to sexual pleasing. I appreciate "mastery" in any skill.

The slave is expected to pleasure Master sexually every day using various sexual and BDSM skills. Sexual climax is not the goal. The goal is to have daily intimate connection.

Master will indicate whether the evening is to be sensual, medium-intense, or edgy-intense. Within those guidelines, the specific sexual and BDSM activity choices are left to slave's creativity, imagination, and skills. At no time will the slave Top Master for the slave's pleasure: the slave is always in service.

slave has a duty to provide aftercare following play, and to alert Master if slave is experiencing Topdrop over the next day or two.

Equipment protocols for SM scenes

As it's hard to anticipate the direction of our SM play, the slave typically sets out the following:

- 3-4 Hatachi-like vibrators (they're all slightly different: they give different sensations)

- 3-4 insertable vibrators, especially the Shabari Halo®

- 1-2 eStim boxes and the box of inserts plus the box of connectors. Sometimes we also put out a box of various sized external eStim pads.

- Box of compression tools (clips and clamps)

- 3-4 sizes/thicknesses of rattan canes

- 4-8 floggers

- Penis pump (that we use vaginally)

- Lube + hand towels + paper towels

As we play in the living room on the couch, equipment is to be placed on the coffee table or on the floor within easy reach.

Protocols for sensual oiled massage

Master loves having oiled massage scenes in front of our fireplace (lit with logs or with candles). This is typically a 90 minutes scene resulting in happy endings for all.

Set-up:

- Massage table + covering sheet (table looks better when covered)

- Bath towel covering most of the sheet (to absorb oil overflow and body fluids)

- Side table on which is the baby bottle warmer (for heating the massage oil) and a Sunbeam® Hot Pot (for heating one or two small towels)

- Lube

- Massage oil (leather-scented body oil, if available)

- Vibrators (anything like a Hitachi Magic Wand® or a Thumper® Sport Percussive Massager)

- Paper towels and hand towels

Ambiance:

- Dim the lights; light candles
- Music: "Woo" music, such as "Shamanic Dreams"
- Optional: smudge the room with a sage stick

Psychological preparation:

- I will inform the slave on the intent of the massage. In a general way, it will either be a "sensations/sexual" massage, an SM play massage, or a true back massage. slave will keep these categories separate.

Tips

- The slave will squirt oil into its hands to test warmth. slave will not squirt the oil directly on Master as that communicates "shortcut" and "hurry" as opposed to sensual connection.

- The slave is to be careful with the hot towels. it may have trouble wringing them out because they're too hot. Applying overly hot towels will break the mood of the scene.

- After one towel has been placed on the back and started to cool, place the second towel on top of it. THIS towel can be much hotter.

- At the slave's discretion, it may turn the scene into a fire massage at this point. A fire massage fits into all three "intent" categories.

- The slave is to spend massage time on hands, fingers, soles of feet...

Protocols when Master is Topping someone

The slave will assist in equipment set-up when Master has set up an SM play date with someone, whether male or female. Master may wish to conduct this scene alone or when the slave is present. In some cases, Master may plan a scene that involves the slave's participation as the co-Top.

In either case, Master will inform the slave of what is needed and what expectation Master has of the slave with respect to the planned scene.

Protocols when Master is playing sexually with other men

Master will occasionally play sexually with other men. Such play will be strictly at Master's instigation; Master will handle all related negotiations. With extremely few exceptions, Master wishes the slave to be present, not only to join in the play (so it is a shared experience), but also for security reasons.

When the slave is present, it is to be supportive and helpful. This may involve providing lube, towels, or condoms, or may involve setting up scene music and preparing snacks and beverages. The slave will follow Master's lead concerning timing and pacing, but will also have the sensitivity to leave the room when the slave senses that its presence is somehow limiting play. The slave will always be attentive to Master's facial and hand gestures in order to help guide the action. Master will signal the slave if Master wishes slave to interrupt the action and provide a break.

There are three general protocols that govern slave's involvement with Master's play with others:

- Participate from the outset: When an afternoon or evening has been planned that involves another man for sexual play, the slave is responsible for all logistics related to setting up the house and establishing a warm and welcoming ambiance.

- Join in after the play has started: With established play partners, Master enjoys scheduling play to start 60-90 minutes before the slave is expected home from a trip or from work. In those scenarios, the slave is to let itself into the house, strip, shower, and join the play.

- Do not participate at all: Once Master trusts the other man/men, Master may agree to private plays sessions. Usually, these will occur when the slave is out of town. Occasionally, Master may wish the slave to occupy itself elsewhere for part or all of the play.

An Allegory for the End

Once upon a time, long ago in Egypt, a Pharaoh called upon his Vizier (essentially, a Prime Minister) to summon the three wisest men in the kingdom. Within the month, the Vizier had arranged the audience. The Pharaoh spoke: "Gentlemen, I am sending you on a Quest. I seek to know what makes things happen. I wish to understand what motivates people to act."

The three men were stunned. They had no idea how to approach answers to these questions. After they were dismissed, they met for days upon days trying to figure out what the Pharaoh could possibly want as a reply. They mapped out a course of study and after many years, got word to the Vizier that they were prepared to present their answer to the Pharaoh.

The next day, the men assembled where they'd been told and the Pharaoh came in. The men said:

"Oh great Master, you asked us to discover and tell you what makes things happen; you asked us to explain the source of individual motivation."

The Pharaoh said: "Oh, yes. That was many years ago. I'd wondered what had become of you. So: what have you found?"

"Great Master, we have written it all out on these papyrus scrolls." They indicated an immense pile of scrolls.
"I don't want to read all that, just explain it to me." Said the Pharaoh.

"Master, the answer is more complex than we can quickly explain."

The Pharaoh, said: "Then go away again until you have shortened your answer." He left the room.

The three men were again left speechless. Their work of many years had not produced the result they intended. They directed their slaves to collect the scrolls and to take them back to their study center.

Two years later, the men again arranged a meeting with the Pharaoh and again presented their findings: "Master, we have now summarized and condensed forty-five scrolls down to two. Here, Master, is the answer to your question about what causes things to happen."

The Pharaoh had his Vizier bring him a scroll. He opened it and read a bit then asked for the second scroll. He looked at it, too. Finally he put it down and turned to the three men.

"Look. I know you're putting your hearts and minds into this project, but you're missing the mark. Let me put some pressure on you. On pain of death, you are to return to your studies and within six months make a verbal presentation that does not take more than five minutes. In that time, you are to explain to me what motivates things to happen."
The men were terrified. They were true scholars who were well known throughout the land. Never before had they felt as humble and worthless. They returned to their studies.

Before the six months were out, they notified the Vizier that they were ready to make a one-sentence summary of their findings. The Vizier told the Pharaoh, of course, and the meeting was arranged for the next day.

The Pharaoh, an optimistic man at heart, gathered his most trusted counselors together to hear what the three men had to say. "This should really be good," he confided to his Vizier.

When bidden to step forward, the man chosen to deliver the summary said: "Great Master, you gave us a profound and difficult task. You have asked us to discover and sum-marize in less than five minutes to core truth about what motivates things to happen."

"Yes," said the Pharaoh, "that is exactly what I commanded. So, then, what is the answer?"

"The answer" said the lead scholar, "is that although we did not believe it possible to summarize that information into one sentence or phrase, we have, at last succeeded. We have determined what causes all things to happen in this kingdom."

"Most excellent," said the Pharaoh turning to his counselors and smiling. "And what might that phrase be?"
"Master," said the lead scholar, "That phrase is: 'As Master wishes.'"

###############################

Bob:

This is your protocol Manual.

You are contracted to serve me as I wish; this Manual explains just that.

When your service conforms perfectly to this Manual, you will be serving as I wish.

Master

Section Four Footnotes
There are no footnotes in Section Four

We wish you green lights, a light breeze on your back, and joy filled days.

The End.

Supplementary Material

The Six Rules of our Relationship

1   **Excited and Eager to be Together**

- When given the choice of spending time with someone else or spending time together, we choose to spend that time together.

- When we are apart the other person is foremost in each others' minds and our actions are intended to help and support one another and the relationship.

    - *If something is offered that we know would displease the other, we will refuse it.*

    - *We will show respect towards one another's wants, needs, and dreams.*

        - *I will let my partner finish their thoughts*

        - *I will listen closely to my partner's requests*

        - *I will put my partner first in my thoughts and actions*

- When people see us together they see our connection/love

- When separated during social settings we are aware of the other person and remain connected through eye contact, touch, and verbal communication.

2   **Inclusive Partnership**

- One's strengths help support the other's weaknesses

- We have the intent to build a life on shared experiences. When one or the other of us has an experience separate from the other, we are eager to share that experience to fulfill our intent to have a transparent relationship.

3   **Motivated to Make Each Activity/Experience Special**

- Yes, we are taking another bath...but this is the first bath we are taking today and we will endeavor to make it different, new, exciting, and special.

4   **Wide range of Interests**

- Willing to grow together and learn new things.

- Building shared memories.

5   **Intellectually Curious** and Eager to Grow Both in Knowledge and in Experience

6   Place the Other High on a Pedestal

- How can both people be on a pedestal? If each partner is working <u>selflessly</u> to give the other person everything they need, they then share the pedestal.

Foundation Reading by Dr. Bob

The Concept of Protocols and Rituals

I realize that some of you reading this book already use protocols daily in your lives; I also realize some of you reading this book strongly oppose using protocols in any way whatsoever.

If you belong to the: "We don't use protocols" school of thought please let me speak with you privately for a moment.

It's not that you don't *use* protocols; it's that you don't *name them* "protocols." You probably have ways you want your partner to cook certain foods, prepare your bed at night, or bring you coffee in the morning. These individual actions (protocols) combine to form the rituals of your life. These everyday actions help focus our attention and intent. Protocols can be your friend; I'm only suggesting you recognize them, label them, and use them to your advantage as bonding tools.

Protocols help you appreciate your partner. They help prevent you from developing habits of taking your partner for granted. They help each of you to demonstrate your awareness and gratitude towards the other. Master is honored through the slave's service; the slave is able to imbue mundane tasks with spiritual meaning. Win/win.

Protocols help to reprogram your brain; they help you to create habits. Protocols don't merely define how you look on the outside; protocols help to shape how you think on the inside. Since protocols are the way Master wants this particular slave to do things, and since people are different from one another, protocols are person-specific. You might think of *using protocols in public* as a way of wearing your beliefs. This raises the question about building public protocols that don't freak out the vanillas yet provide the constant connection and bonding these kinds of relationships represent.

Protocols force you into the "act-as-if" structure. The structure of your relationship has everything to do with your mindset and the authority system you're using. For example, protocols will differ dramatically in the context of a Leader/follower team model, or in the context of a paramilitary/hierarchical model, or in the context of a Daddy/supportive model. The point is, you can build protocols into any authority-based relationship system and use them both to recognize the authority imbalance and to honor the relationship.

Partners in non-structured relationships (marriage or BF/GF) often strive for a power-equal relationship. In such environments, each partner has to put up with some of the petty idiosyncrasies of the other, as neither person has the authority to require the other to change their behavior: that's the deal. Although the way one person does something may annoy or bother the other partner, the rules of most authority-equal relationships require the annoyed partner to get used to the behavior they don't like.

Unlike power-equal relationships, Master has undisputed authority over the slave's behavior and actions. In that light, Master can build protocols and simply prohibit unwanted behavior and actions. At least theoretically, slave is motivated to limit its behavior and actions to those that please Master—and thus support the relationship. Although we're back to the "It's good to be king" model of M/s, we're also back to a couple living harmoniously.

Some people say they don't like protocols because they believe the protocol will remove the "fun" from the relationship; now, there will now be a lot of work. This attitude arises because we've associated "work" as something *not fun*. But consider this: when we pick up a tool and go to work (or toy and play) during an SM scene—that's fun and filled with scene protocols you haven't yet named.

Protocols and rituals can help to make your world special.

As you've already read, they can be used to elevate your daily activities from the mundane to something memorable. You can elevate protocols to rituals and ceremonies to celebrate anything in your life: waking up in the morning, being dressed and ready to go to work. Once at work, you can develop protocols to help you to mindfully begin your day while recognizing the very special M/s life you are privileged to live.

You can build actions of gratitude into your day; you can have protocols for recognizing fellow workers or panhandlers on the street. You're alive; you live in a free country; we're not at war; you have a home. Beyond that, you have a partner who is dedicated either to serve you or to protect and care for you.

What else do you want, exactly?

Now, there's a secret involved with turning daily protocols into rituals. The very act of engaging in a ritual or ceremony affirms consent by both Master and slave. When the two (or more) of you perform rituals, each person is really saying something to the other: Master is affirming that the slave is a cherished asset and the slave is affirming that they continue to consent to serve and obey. Thus, the more rituals you can build into your relationship, the more often you are solidifying the bond between you.

Hence the expression that I wrote out some years ago: When the relationship gets into trouble, revert to protocols.

Anticipatory Service

Perfect service anticipates needs and fills them before the other person quite realizes they had the need. This is one of the goals of our personal relationship.

I've made up a little story to illustrate the point.

***

We all know about bad service. You're dining out. The waiter brought your water. At some point, you've emptied your water glass and you're waiting for a refill. No one notices so you sit and wait. Ultimately, you may get fed up and get up to find water. I've had to do this a time or two, and I've even had a waiter get upset with me for doing it. Anyway, you sit back down and finish your meal. Bad service and all. You contemplate not leaving a tip.

Good service is when your glass is empty and a waiter walks by, you catch their attention and ask for some water. They bring it. Good service.

But there is another kind of service: exemplary service: magical service. Your glass is half full and you're engaged in conversation. You reach for your glass and discover that someone filled it without your noticing. You smile. It makes you happy. In this restaurant, servers have been trained in anticipatory service. It's magical. You contemplate leaving a larger tip than usual.

Anticipatory service is more than good service. It is more than great service. It is an attitude. The person providing the service has a unique attitude. They are watching, expecting you to need something. They deliver it right before you even notice you need to ask. When you feel that your glass is heavier than before, you get a charge from their attitude and it makes you happy. It builds trust. You feel respected.

Setting a Formal Table

Menus

If you're interested in playing with protocols at this level, you have two choices for menus. One is a single menu that is mounted on card stock and is standing in a small picture-holding tripod and the other is a menu printed on card stock and placed directly on the dinner plate (presuming you place napkins to the left of the dinner plate, as we do.)

Even as we are preparing this protocol manual in June, 2016, we are building a protocol to prepare dinner menus for evenings when we are Dining In.

I've included and example of a standing menu in the Supplementary material.

When we are dining formally, we follow the traditional order of service for four or five-course meals.

Four courses:

- Seafood cocktail (white wine)
- Soup
- Entrée (red wine) – not if it is salmon
- Cheese and fruit (dessert wine)

Five courses: Same as above but add the salad course after the entrée. As a footnote to history, in the British Military Services, the traditional formal meal includes standing prime rib roast and Yorkshire pudding.

Rolls, coffee, mints

Quick overview: While bread is optional, dinner rolls are always served at formal affairs. However, using bread plates for rolls is optional and depends upon space at Table. Coffee is always served at formal dinners. Mints are frequently served after the final course.

Ambiance

In general, flowers improve the look of the table. Elaborate floral arrangements are THE hallmark of a formal dinner. However, take care not to block one guest's view of another guest with a flower arrangement. If dining at a small table, a small floral arrangement or a bowl of mixed fruit may serve as the centerpiece—or place single flowers in individual vases at each place.

Candlelight adds intimacy to a dinner. The size and style of the candlesticks depend on the occasion itself, but they should never be too grandiose.

Cutlery

Flatware is laid on the table according to use, starting on the outside of the place setting and working toward the plate. Forks are placed to the left of the plate, except that seafood forks are placed to the *right of the spoon, tines up*.

A fork is provided for each course unless one is expected to eat the course with a spoon. When in doubt, ask me. The usual flatware placement presumes that the salad is a first course (informal dinner). So, if the meal includes salad, main, and dessert courses served in this order, the salad fork, dinner fork, and dessert fork will be placed in the same order to the left side of the dinner plate. When salad is served following the main course (formal dinner), the salad fork is placed next to the plate.

The various knives are placed immediately to the right of the plate, also in the order of the dish being served, from the outside toward the inside. Salad and dessert knives are provided if they're likely to be needed for cutting to-matoes or wedges of lettuce in the salad course or fruit in the dessert course. The spoons are placed to the right of all the knives, again in the order of the courses for which they're needed, again from the outside toward the inside.

Teaspoons (or the larger place spoons) on the informal lun-cheon or dinner table are used for soup or fruit that is served in cups. Teaspoons on the breakfast table are for grapefruit, cereals, and the like. Before serving tea or coffee, teaspoons are placed on the saucers at the right of the handles.

- At formal dinners, dessert spoons and/or forks are brought in on the dessert plate. Fork on the left, spoon on the right.

- At informal meals, the dessert spoon and/or fork may be placed on the table, centered above the dinner plate.

I will inform you if I am intending to serve a dinner role. If so, you will set out the bread plates to the left of the fork with the individual butter spreader placed across the plate's top edge. If we will be serving antipasto (an appetizer usually consisting of an assortment of foods such as smoked meats, cheese, fish, and vegetables), then the slave will place a plate smaller than the dinner plate on top of the dinner plate (that, itself, is on top of the charger plate. Yes, I know that charger plates are customarily removed when the main course is served, but I like the look of the charger plate beneath our dinner plates). Use the same setup if we're beginning the meal with pasta rather than an antipasto: the smaller plate is placed on top of the dinner plate.

Napkins

Napkin size varies with the function. While we use 22" and 24" napkins, I expect you to know the correct sizes for napkins used in various settings:

- 24" square: very formal dinner

- 18–22" square: less formal multi-course meal

- 12" x 20" (called "lapkins") are for a buffet service where a one-dish menu is eaten from the lap

- 14–16" square: luncheon service

- 12" square (held under a tea plate): used for afternoon tea

- Cocktail napkins: when folded properly in quarters, are about rd the size of the luncheon napkin

Water pitcher

Those unused to providing more formal dinners sometimes overlook water. The water pitcher—usually made of cut glass—contributes to the air of old-fashioned formality.

Refer to your "pre-dinner checklist" (see Supplements) for our protocols concerning when to fill the glasses with water and when to add the three ice cubes. As the pitcher of water also contains ice and will "sweat" throughout the evening, it must be placed on a plate to avoid creating an ever-widening water spot on the tablecloth. The water pitcher will remain on the table throughout the meal.

Serving dishes

The sizes of serving dishes and platters vary as a function of the number of guests you routinely serve. You will gener-ally need serving dishes appropriate to serve the following.

- Vegetable dishes

- Soft dishes such as fruit compote (bowl required)

- Fruits and desserts (shallow bowl required)

- Bread tray or basket

- Sauceboat or gravy boat with matching ladle

- Small oval platter for meats or fish

- Large oval platter for large roasts (or cold meats at a buffet)

- Round platter or cake stand (a cake plate on a ped-estal) for serving pies, cakes, cookies etc.

Salt and pepper

It is a hallmark of a formal dinner that each guest has individual salt and pepper shakers at their place setting.

Wine caddy

To avoid getting spots of red wine on the tablecloth, bottles are placed in a wine caddy. White wine bottles are placed in the insulated chiller. The chiller is set on a side table. Because the chiller is designed to hold the entire bottle and is insulated, it does not require a plate beneath it (as would a wine bucket).

Place cards

I'll tell you which of our place-card holders we'll use with company. The slave has discretion to select the holder it prefers when we are dining alone.

Menu placement

If we're using menu cards, place them flat, directly centered on the dinner plate. You'll have to use this placement, as the name card is set into a holder. A formal dinner setting mandates that each guest have their own menu.

Levels of Dress

- Dressy and semi-formal evening dress: Black tie or Military Mess Dress. May not be worn before 6 pm. Black tuxedo jackets or white dinner jackets are appropriate. For women, cocktail dresses or floor-length gowns are appropriate.

- Full formal: White tie and tails. Boutonnieres other than white or red carnations may be worn in the left buttonhole. After 6 pm except during the summer: Tails for men and floor-length black gown for women.

- <u>Family Ceremony:</u> Cutaway jackets (black or gray) are reserved for very special Family ceremonies (or steam-punk events, when worn with a top hat).

Miscellaneous dressing issues

- <u>Boutonnieres:</u> Boutonnieres are NOT routinely used within our Family. (As an aside, do NOT wear a boutonniere when wearing military decorations.)

- <u>Dress handkerchief:</u> Family Protocols call for a red or black silk handkerchief used with tuxedo and tails — this is an optional item. Other handkerchief colors may be worn during the day and, if chosen, should blend with one's tie.

- <u>Medals and awards:</u> Considering that we have not had the honor of serving in the military, we are cautious about the use of service medals for fetish dress. slave may wear a gold-colored hand-cuff tie-tack on its mess dress lapels.

If our guests have earned service medals or awards, the protocol we recommend is: miniature medals are worn with Mess Dress, Semiformal Dress and Dress Whites. Ribbons are worn with Mess Dress, Evening Dress and Full Formal.

Notes about Table service

Service at a formal table must be efficient, quiet and unob-trusive. Nothing is ever taken directly from a slave's hands. Drinks are served on trays and food is served from a platter.

The service must be consistent among our guests or they might think something is missing. The slave will take care to serve everybody the same: you can't serve Master differently or guests will notice they're not getting the "special service." Everybody needs to feel they are special.

Formal plated service means that the slave will have put food on the dinner plate in the kitchen and brings it to the dining room and serves it to the guest from their left side, using its left hand.

Informal plated service only differs in that the slave may carry two plated dishes at one time, one in each hand. The slave will only use its left had for placing a plate in front of a guest, so after the first plate is served, the slave will transfer the second plate from its right to its left hand before serving the next guest.

Once everyone has been served their main course, the slave will then return to the kitchen to retrieve trays of condiments. If this is a formal setting, the slave will carry only one condiment at a time. If this is an informal setting, the slave may carry one condiment container in each hand.

The slave will be gloved for formal service and ungloved for informal service.

Table-clearing and cleanup protocols

China plates are not to be stacked when removing them from the table. Carry one plate per hand per trip. Remove dishes to the kitchen and soak them in the rubber tub that fits inside the sink. Take care to be as quiet as possible.

Late-night snack after a formal meal

When the "after party" continues late into the evening, it is customary to serve late-night bites to guests who stick around, or to guests as they leave.

If we are entertaining late and offering more food after the documented dessert, these items are *not* to be included on the menu card, and are *not* served at Table. However (if there is room) the slave may include a single line at the end of the menu, "Late bites offered after 11 p.m." or something similar.

We have established two customs with respect to serving additional foods to guests who stay late:

- Serve warmed Brie and pears (use our grey 6" dessert plates). Offer espresso, either caffeinated or decaf (accompanied by half-and-half in the creamer and sugar cubes in the sugar jar).

- Prepare and distribute to departing guests a "favor bag." I'll give you ample time and resources to prepare these during the day.

(Note: Even at formal dinners, these items are not served at the tables where guests are seated.)

Sterling care

My favorite resource for all things silver: www.herman-silver.com/care.htm. However, here are the basics: additional tactics for dealing with damage follow:

- Hand-wash, then dry right away

- Do NOT put silver in the dishwasher. The high heat and chemicals used in machine dishwashing are very hard on sterling. Never soak sterling knives: it can loosen knife handles. In a general way, soaking sterling silver can roughen the silver's surface. After the meal, wash silverware and silver serving vessels as soon as possible. Use hot water and Dawn® detergent. Rinse with hot water.

Repeatedly washing silver in the dishwasher causes a whitish haze on the flatware. This is because of the alkali in the detergent. This white haze is hard to remove, often requiring professional attention. You may also find that you're getting black spots on your silver if any stainless steel comes in contact with it during the wash cycle. The black spots are caused by an electrolytic reaction between the two dissimilar metals. Worst of all, the heat in a dishwasher can loosen the cement that fastens knife blades to their handles, or even make the cement expand

Protect between uses

It's easy to keep air-borne contaminants away from silver; just pop a few 3M® anti-tarnish strips into your flatware drawer, and change them periodically. If you'd rather, a drawer can be lined in Pacific Silvercloth.™ It will reduce tarnishing. Silver chests are lined in this material, too.

If you can arrange it, it's better to store silver in rows, laying each piece on its side, rather than stacking. This minimizes scratching. For long-term storage, Ziploc™ bags are great, but *never use plastic wrap*. It can bond itself to silver, requiring professional removal. *Never use a rubber band around silver*; it will leave black tarnish wherever it touches.

No silver dips. Ever.

Silver dips work by a chemical action that is hard on silver, and can damage pieces if it is left on too long. Silver dips are also capable of soaking into knife handles and hollow parts like teapot feet, creating expensive problems.

You will use Wright's Silver Cream™ for polishing silver. Follow the directions on the container. Rinse after polishing and dry using a polishing cloth designed for that purpose.

Fixing damaged silver

Use a rouge-based polish to remove deep tarnish and light scratches. I prefer Wenol (pronounced VEE-knoll) but you may also use Simichrome™. These polishes will bring up a deep luster on silver. Note: these are too abrasive for regular polishing. Only use them for restoration purposes. Polish using a soft cotton cloth. Wash the silver after polishing to remove polish residue.

Example of a Recommitment Ceremony

In Bob's former relationship they would preform a *recommitment ceremony* each evening, bringing focus, intent and beauty forward into their Evening.

> Master: "What have we here?"
>
> slave: "Your slave, Master"
>
> Master: "So it is. And what in the world shall I do with a slave?"
>
> slave: "Take it and keep it as yours, if it pleases you, Master."
>
> Master: "And why should I do such a thing?"
>
> slave: "Because you own me, Master, because this slave loves to serve you with grace and elegance, and so you can fuck my brains out whenever you choose."
>
> Master: "Ah, slave. These are good reasons. I will accept you. You may continue."

Upon Master's signal, slave rolls up (backwards) in one fluid motion to standing position.

Once this is over, they would shower and change and the slave prepares dinner.

Additional Material About Dining and Diner Protocols

Sample eMail sent to guests for a small dinner party

Hello "X,"

I have put the 15th on our calendar. Arriving at 6:30 and dinner at 8.

I still need to know if you two have any food allergies or food preferences. For example, are either of you sensitive to onions or peppers? How do you feel about blue cheese dressing?

I'd like to give you a heads-up about our dinner protocols so you're not caught off guard. These are actions that support our relationship and we perform them nightly.

- My slave will seat me and then you may sit in the manner that supports your relationship

- We will have a brief centering ceremony (a connection and focus for us). This does not require your attention, just letting you know that it will occur.

- My slave will serve the food. It will serve me first as Host, then serve you as our senior guest. It will then serve your girl. The slave will plate its food in the kitchen and serve itself after we are served.

- My slave will serve the wine in the same order.

- We will have two toasts: slave will give a toast to thank you for joining us and then slave will ring a bell and we will offer a toast our Leather brethren.

- I will invite you to begin eating (in the manner it supports your relationship). I will give slave its first bite before it is allowed to eat freely.

While we eat formally, we are not formal eating. Sometimes one gets caught up in the have-to-do's and miss the fun. Our protocols are designed to bring fun and focus to dinner. Frequently we eat dinner without thinking about what we are doing in vanillaland.

We like to dress up for dinner. This can be to whatever level you are comfortable from formal (tux and evening gown) to semi-formal (suit and party dress) to casual (suit pants with a button down shirt and skirt or slacks) to fetish (role-play clothing) to Leather formal (what you would wear to a Leather banquet). Again, the intent is to have an experience that is like no other. Please let me know the level of dress and formality you would enjoy experiencing with us.

As we get closer to the date I will turn the logistics over to my slave who will send you an email with directions to our home. He will also answer any last-minute questions. This is also part of our relationship structure.

We look forward to seeing you both on November 15th.

Jen and Bob

Table Manners (in general)

Your mother was right: table manners DO count. Here is my version of a "critical list." My slave is expected to know and follow these rules.

Foundation rules

- Do not bring your cocktail glass to the table.

- In our home, dinner is a special time. It is not a place for preaching or being assertive or argumentative. Dignity will never go out of style.

- It is very impolite to season your food before you have tasted it. It is an insult to the chef who prepared the meal and thereby, it is also an insult to your host.

- Cut only enough food for the next mouthful.

- Do not speak with food in your mouth. Chew with your mouth closed and don't smack or crunch.

- Don't slump at the table. Sit forward in your chair, showing your interest in the conversation.

- Avoid curling your feet around the chair legs; simi-larly, avoid stretching your feet out under the table.

- If food spills off your plate, use your silverware to pick it up and place it on the right hand side of your plate.

Jam, butter, bread and passing dishes

- If butter and/or jam is served, after transferring a small portion from the serving dish to your bread plate, spread the butter on individual bites of bread, not on the entire side of the bread or roll.

- Break bread and rolls in half with your fingers, then into single-bite pieces that you place in your mouth. Do NOT cut breads with a knife. Do NOT take a bite from the broken piece of bread or roll and place the remainder back onto the bread plate.

- Take a passed dish (or bread basket) from the per-son and thank them in a clear and deliberate voice. *Do not select an item from the dish (or basket) while the other guest is holding it.*

- If something is slightly out of reach, ask that it be passed to you; do NOT start to rise out of your seat to reach for it. Do not reach in front of anyone else at the table to get something even if it is within your reach.

Fingers, lips, hands and elbows

- When you are not eating, keep your hands in your lap, or resting on the table (with only your wrists on the edge of the table).

- Keep arms and elbows OFF the table in the U.S. (until you have completed each course, at which point it is generally considered acceptable to lean on the table in order to hear conversations better). The exception in the U.S. is that between courses you may momentarily rest your forearms on the table so long as you do not turn your back on your partner. (Note: On the European Continent, it is customary to rest your forearms on the table so that your hands are in clear view. But, that's because the Europeans don't want seatmates holding hands out of view. I've lived there and know this custom well.)

- Never lick your fingers after they have contacted food; your napkin is for that purpose.

- Never rub your lips with a napkin, pat them. Pat your mouth with your napkin before drinking from your wine or water glass to avoid leaving oils, grease or food particles on the rim of the glass.

- If food gets between your teeth while you are eating, try to dislodge the item without leaving the table. Eat what you dislodge: never wipe the dislodged food on your napkin. If you are unable to dislodge the food and you believe it is visible to others, excuse yourself from the table and resolve the situation in a bathroom. Do not leave the table unless it is absolutely necessary to do so.

- If you MUST remove something from your mouth (olive pit, piece of gristle) cover your mouth with your napkin, cup your other hand in front of your mouth to receive the rejected item. Place it as unobtrusively as you can upon your dinner plate.

Meal's end

- Monitor eating progress of others at the table. Speed up or slow down, as necessary. Once Master finishes eating, the slave is, by definition, finished with dinner.

- When you finish your meal, DON'T push your plate back. Leave it alone.

- The slave(s) will remove any crumbs that have fallen onto the table. Don't touch anything that has fallen onto the table surface.

- If you have to get up to leave the table temporarily, place your napkin in your chair.

- When the meal is over, place your napkin to the left of the dinner plate. NEVER place your napkin directly on your used dinner plate.

Table manners—some specifics
How to use your flatware—American Style–cutting food
Once you pick up a piece of cutlery, you should never put it back on the table. (Exception: if a knife rest has been provided, you may place your knife there between courses.)

- Fork: The fork is held in the left hand, tines down, index finger on back of fork's stem pinning the food (such as a piece of meat). Do not overload your fork with food; dainty is good.

- Knife: Hold your knife in the right hand, index finger on back of knife blade. Cut one single piece of meat, use the knife if necessary to unpin the food from the fork, and then put the knife down onto the plate — blade facing toward the center of the plate. Unless you eat in the left-handed "European Style," transfer the fork to right hand — tines up — push the fork tines underneath, not into, the piece of food to pick it up. You may use your knife as a "pusher" if you need help getting foodstuffs onto your fork. Put the food in your mouth and replace the fork on plate, tines up, below your knife, which should be resting diagonally across the upper right rim of the plate.

- Spoons: The *dessertspoon* is longer than the *teaspoon* and is placed on the dessert plate at formal or informal meals. The *teaspoon* should appear in the saucer of the coffee cup, when served. The *soupspoon* is longer than the dessertspoon OR the teaspoon and has an oval bowl. It is only used with crème soups.

Remember to use a soupspoon by dipping it towards the back of the bowl, starting with the side of the spoon that's farthest away from you. You fill the tilted spoon by pushing it away from you towards the back of the bowl. This technique will help you keep your soup off of your clothes, because any drip will be more likely to travel forward underneath the spoon and land in your mouth than to fall directly off the bottom of the spoon.

Try to avoid scraping the bottom of the soup bowl. When you are done with the spoon, place it on the soup plate to the right-hand side of the bowl.

- Do not blow on hot liquids to cool them; stir them with a spoon and then test the temperature by taking a small spoonful of the liquid.

- For clear soups only, do NOT place the entire spoon inside your mouth; sip the soup from the side of the spoon. Do not slurp the liquid. (For cream soups, you may place the entire spoon in your mouth.)

- Leave the soupspoon IN the soup bowl but do not leave the soupspoon in a bouillon cup or a cream soup bowl.

- You are obliged to take (and eat) a small portion from every serving dish. Nothing may be passed by.

How to hold wine and liquor glasses
For long-stemmed water and white wine glasses, grip the stem of the glass in such a way as not to warm the glass and, by extension, the wine. That is, don't cup the

cupped part of a white wine or water glass. Red wine may be cupped with fingers because warmed wine releases more aroma/bouquet.

Tumblers are held near the base. Brandy snifters are cupped in the palm of the hand in order to warm the brandy

Toasts

Everyone stands when a toast is offered at a formal meal, everyone will STAND *unless* you are the person *receiving the toast* — in which case, you remain seated while everyone else stands. If this is an **informal** meal, everyone remains seated while the toast is offered.

Finger Bowls

These are "finger bowl protocols."

- Set up: This will be a small china or silver bowl two thirds full of warm water, usually with a piece of lime or lemon floating in it. (The acid in the citric fruit will help to remove grease.)

- Do not pick up the slice of lemon; that is frowned upon.

- Move your fingertips briefly within the water, then bring your napkin up with your other hand to meet your fingers. Dry your fingers beneath the table with your hands in your lap.

Table Manners – Restaurant Dining

My slave will follow these additional rules when we are dining at a restaurant.

- The slave will seat Master, remain standing behind Master, and conduct our "centering ritual."

- The slave will remove silverware from the napkin, polish the silverware, place the tableware in its correct location, then unfold and spread the napkin on Master's lap.

- The slave will then take its seat and attend until Master has reviewed the wine, cocktail, or appetizer menu.

- The slave will not speak directly to the waitstaff, but convey any preferences to Master, who will then order for the slave and convey preferences to the waitstaff.

- The slave will be eating one-half of whatever meal I choose. I will make my choice after consulting the slave, but am certainly not bound by the slave's preferences.

- As previously mentioned, taste first, season second. In the world of business, this suggests that you reach conclusions without assessing the facts.

- If you do not like the food or the way it was prepared, keep this information to yourself unless a food-safety issue is involved. I *do not* like food discussed at the table. We are dining out to have a good time, not to discuss the meal.

The slave's pre-dinner checklist when guests are coming

Instruction

You shall re-read "The slave's Rules of Decorum once guests arrive" every time you use this checklist. Please check them off once you've read them.

This form is due back to me BEFORE guests arrive.

Day before we are having guests

- ☐ Check wine and liquor needs with Master, especially our supply of Port

- ☐ Coordinate shopping list with Master. Ask about:

  - ☐ Plate garnishing greens we may need

  - ☐ Desserts we may need, particularly if serving sorbet

  - ☐ Anything we needs fresh for the meal (dinner rolls?)

- ☐ Confirm any equipment rentals.

Morning Preparations. These must be complete before meal preparations

General house prep

Kitchen

- ☐ Nothing will (yet) be set out on any kitchen surface. Nothing.

- ☐ All surfaces will have been cleaned with a spray cleaner. Stains will have been removed by combining the liquid cleaner with a powdered cleanser.

☐ The floor will have been cleaned within the past 24 hours or must now be re-cleaned.

Living Room

☐ Sweep the floors first, and then clean them using the Hoover Floormate.

☐ Verify that nothing is left out in the living room.

☐ Verify that everything is positioned the way I like them.

☐ Wicks on all candles in the room have been shortened.

☐ Fireplace is set with a fire log or candles (If necessary, clean soot out of fireplace).

☐ Be sure all the water for cut flowers is clear (not cloudy) and that all indoor plants have adequate water.

Dining Table

☐ If necessary, remove flowers from that table—prepare centerpiece

☐ Set the table with as many additional settings as we need for our guests

☐ Double-check each table setting by sitting it each chair to verify:

  ☐ Dinner plate is centered on the charger plate

  ☐ Cutlery are parallel with one another and are equidistant from the table edge

☐ Water and wine glasses are spaced equally and lined up

☐ Polish all glasses, plates, and flatware being put out for guests

☐ Confirm size/type of wine glasses match tonight's dinner and change if necessary

☐ Print place cards and place on table according to Master's instructions

☐ Confirm that all napkins are fresh, pressed, and correctly folded

☐ Check chair positions for each place

Setup—Guest bathroom

☐ Replace toilet paper roll with fresh roll

☐ Check that the box of facial tissue is reasonably full

☐ Wipe down the bathroom counter and sink

☐ Clean the toilet bowl

☐ Verify that hand towels are fresh

☐ Verify that fresh soap is in the soap dish

☐ Verify that the bathroom floors/rugs are clean

Afternoon preparations

☐ Food preparation, starting time set as instructed by Master

☐ Place cheeses on serving trays two hours before guests arrive so they can come to room temperature

☐ The name of each cheese will be displayed on individual cheese labels

☐ All food prep has been completed 90 minutes before guest arrival time

Activities beginning 75 minutes before guests are to arrive

☐ The slave showers 75 minutes before setup

☐ The slave is Dressed 45 minutes before setup

Activities beginning 45 minutes before guests are to arrive

The slave presents itself to Master and confirms it is ready to begin preparing for guests. The slave has 45 minutes to complete this part of the checklist

Food prep

☐ Any last-minute food prep fits into this time slot.

General setup

☐ All overhead lights have been correctly set to a soft feel

☐ Appetizers are plated in kitchen and placed on counter or in refrigerator.

☐ Red wine bottles are opened and breathing 30min before guests arrive

☐ White wine is either already chilled or in the chiller

Appetizers and Coffee Table

☐ All necessary serving utensils for appetizers are set out, including crackers/apples

☐ If we are serving mixed drinks, glasses are set out along with red cocktail napkins

☐ If we are serving Port, be sure the decanter is adequately filled and Port glasses are polished

Dining Table

☐ Water glasses are half filled. Ice will be added later.

Kitchen Area

☐ One spare dinner plate is on the kitchen island

☐ All silver dinner-serving utensils are now placed on kitchen island

☐ Condiments are in bowls, stored in refrigerator—applesauce, etc.

Activities beginning 15 minutes before guests are to arrive

☐ Light fire in fireplace (or candles in fireplace, depending on season)

☐ Light other room candles

☐ Turn on the initial background music

☐ Double-check room lights. Be sure that the main kitchen lights are off

☐ Bring appetizers to living room

☐ Put three ice cubes in each water glass

☐ Turn Harvey on and set up with correct music: press "pause" button.

☐ Pre-dinner music is set up and playing quietly

☐ The "thunder storm" track is playing on the iPod

The slave's ongoing monitoring responsibilities

Appetizer phase

Your job is to be on-point so far as wine/cocktail/water glasses are concerned. **If you can, clear off used plates and the appetizers before you start Harvey.**

Dinner Phase

- Your job is to closely monitor *everyone's* glasses and plates. It is not my job to tell you. I expect to see your eyes sweeping the table every few minutes, as the meal hits mid-stride

- Once everyone has finished and we are speaking and sipping wine, I will indicate when you are to clear the table.

The slave's Rules of Decorum once guests arrive

- If we have discussed some topic that I do NOT want brought up, don't bring it up

- You are to closely monitor body language and be quick to change subjects if a guest appears uncomfortable. Indications: guest is leaning *back* instead of forward; legs and/or arms are crossed; guest is not interacting very much.

- You are to listen closely *and follow* when I suddenly change the subject. Under no circumstances are you to bring the conversation back to the prior topic.

- Our job is to ensure that the guests leave feeling that we were attentive. This means drawing them out, not entertaining them with our life or stories--unless asked and I signal you that you may do so. Your guide is: "It's better to be interested than interesting."

- Be *extremely* attentive to any guest lowering his/her head as a point is made. This is an unconscious indication that this person strongly disagrees with you and is trying not to say anything.

- You will *always* start serving in the order of precedence, beginning with the senior man or woman. This person is likely to be seated across from me.

- When I have finished my plate, the meal is over. You will not ask to clear the table, you will rise and escort me to the living room.

- ____ I have re-read this list carefully and will follow it in letter and spirit

Example of a formal dinner menu

Miscellaneous Checklists

Travel checklist

Trip Location: _____

Trip Dates: _____ Cash obtained for this trip: _____

☐ Flights: Airline: _____ Conf.#: _____ Cost: _____

☐ Boarding pass(es) printed _____

☐ Hotel: Name: _____ Dates covered: _____

    Phone #: _____ Conf.#: _____ Cost: _____

    Hotel address_____

☐ Car rental: Company: _____ Conf.#: _____ Cost: _____

    Rental company phone # _____

Basics

☐ "Weather conditions" report covering all travel days

☐ Attach a sheet that includes all relevant driving directions and maps

☐ If entertainment reserved, include all driving directions, times, confirm #s

☐ Print boarding pass

Travel snacks

☐ Teabags, Sweetener, Creamer

☐ Nuts, raisins, dates, apples, etc.

☐ Liquor

Miscellaneous

☐ Business cards in wallet plus extra cards in computer case

☐ Gift for the host/hostess?

☐ Black shoe-polish can + applicator rag + polishing nylon + latex gloves

Packing issues

☐ Remove scissors from toiletries bag

☐ Rx pills and lip balm / suntan lotion / bug spray are in the toiletries bag

☐ Notebook and pen in the computer bag

☐ Small flashlight

☐ Socks and underwear

☐ Bathing suit

☐ Evening clothes: black dress slacks, dress shoes, black dress shirt and jacket

☐ Day clothing and shoes/boots

☐ Jackets, raingear (per weather report)

☐ Jacket for flight

☐ Play equipment, as needed

☐ Wall and/or car chargers for cameras, phones and computers

☐ Verify that cell phone, computer battery, and camera batteries are charged

☐ Reading glasses

Guest logs

We keep two logs: an "event log" (to keep track of events we host) and a guest log containing information about the guests. Both are Word files. The event log is in chronological order and the guest log is in alphabetical order

Event Log

- Event date:
- Event theme:
- Event format (informal, picnic, formal, play party, etc.):
- Level of formality (casual, dressy, fetish, formal):
- Attendees:
  - a
  - b
  - c
  - d

Guest Log

Basic information

- Fet name
- Scene name
- Legal name
- Partner's name
- How do we know this person
- Physical address (for sending a "thank you" card)
- Email address
- Right or left handed
- Power structure (D/s; M/s...)

Stated food preferences

- Food restrictions they told us about in advance
- Food allergies
- Wine (especially what they, themselves, brought)
- How they take their coffee if they take it
- Favorite cocktail

What did we serve (including reactions to it)

- Appetizers
- Wine
- Main course
- Sides
- Desert

Date they came dinner

- Special occasion?
- What did they bring?
- What did we wear?
  - Master
  - slave

Describe the evening: describe the conversation and tone / temper / mood of the evening

- Summarize high points, especially strengths the guest brought to the evening.
- Comments on table manners and general decorum,
- If we played, describe that.
- Why would we want to invite them back?
- Why would THEY want to come back?
- What would we do differently next time?

The Happy Ending

A Hug Certificate for You!

If I could catch a rainbow
I would do it just for you
And share with you its beauty
On the days you're feeling blue.

If I could build a mountain
You could call your very own;
A place to find serenity,
A place to be alone.

If I could take your troubles
I would toss them in the sea,
But all these things, I'm finding,
Are impossible for me.

I cannot build a mountain
Or catch a rainbow fair,
But let me be what I know best,
A friend who's always there.

Life is a coin,
you can spend it anyway you wish,
but you can only spend it once.

About the Authors

M. Jen Fairfield

Jen Fairfield is an experienced communicator. She's been forced into this role both as the daughter and wife of military officers, but also in her profession.

Jen has extensive experience managing discussions and interpersonal communications both in her personal and work lives. A master teacher, she created (and taught for five years) a state-certified adult-education course in her professional field. In her work life, Jen has (for over 25 years) been called upon daily to ensure clear (and positive) communication in doctor/patient settings.

Over the past five years, Jen has found her calling attending conferences and workshops, reading books, and working closely with Dr. Rubel as he has been researching, writing books, and making presentations both inside and outside the US.

Jen augments Bob's thinking and writing by bringing a fresh vision. With a 20-year age gap between them, they have very different views on many subjects. However, she and Bob use these disagreements as opportunities to explore topics very differently than either of them would have on our own. They both grew from these (often contentious) discussions.

Jen has been instrumental in shaping this particular book. She is responsible for the way the concepts are grouped and flow. While not NLP-certified, she has had ample exposure to the concepts and principals that she naturally applies to conversations.

Jen has a point-of-view about communication: First, she believes that the cultural connotation of words— more than the words themselves—fill sentences with the graphic details that form the basis of one's "social intelligence" (or SI). Second, she has a backbone of steel and believes that we communicate equally through our actions as through our words. She believes that what you do is who you are. She would say: "Your word is your bond: your honor is based on your word."

Ms Fairfield's eidetic memory has been one the most valuable gifts she brought to her union with Dr. Rubel. Much to the benefit of his writing, her memory enables her to assimilate an amazingly diverse range of ideas on all kinds of topics and present them with depth and clarity. This book has benefitted from this ability.

Robert J. Rubel, PhD

Overview

Dr. Rubel is an educa-
tional sociologist and
researcher by training
and an author, lecturer
and photographer by
choice. For the last
decade, he has written
over a dozen books,
mostly on communi-
cations and relation-
ship issues of inter-
est to those who live
in the world of alter-
native sexuality. As

a national presenter on things kinky, Dr. Rubel has
presented to over a hundred clubs/events worldwide
and (at 71) continues to present at national conferences 5-8 times a year.

More detail

Bob graduated from the International School of
Geneva, in Geneva Switzerland. He took his under-
graduate degree at Colorado State University in Ft.
Collins, Colorado.

Immediately after college he taught high school
English for three years in South-Central Los Angeles.
Returning to graduate school, he earned an EdM
(Boston University) and PhD (as a Ford Fellow at the

University of Wisconsin, Madison) in the area edu-
cational policy studies with a minor in criminology.
After serving a stint as a Visiting Fellow at the U.S.
Department of Justice's National Institute of Justice,
he formed a 501(c)(3) foundation that specialized
in crime prevention in public schools. He ran the
National Alliance for Safe Schools for 17 years. During
part of that period, he helped create the American
Association of Woodturners. For its first three years,
Bob served as its Administrator.

Robert has extensive management experience with
non-profit organizations and at one point was designated a Certified Association Executive through the
American Society of Association Executives. He is a
heavily published author and has served as founder
and managing editor of two national quarterlies, one
for school police/security directors, and one for his
beloved art-form of woodturning

Mid-career
In his mid-40s, Bob decided to change careers utterly
and joined a stock brokerage and future brokerage
firm in Washington, D.C. Within six months, he was
made a Principal of the futures brokerage side of the
firm, and five months after that, was asked to serve
as CEO. He ran the company until, four years later,
a close friend asked him to return to Austin to help
start a new company.

Later years

After five years, Bob retired to pursue his fascination with the world of alternative sexuality, throwing himself into the literature of the field as though it were an academic study. After publishing six books in the 2006-9 period, Bob began lecturing and presenting throughout North America (with brief forays abroad). From 2007-2016, he has presented at nearly a hundred conferences, usually making two or more presentations per event. Most of his topics concern the nearly unending intricacies of communication.

Bob's passion for researching, writing, and lecturing about communication challenges began in 2006 when his then-partner pointed out that he undoubtedly had Asperger Syndrome. Ultimately, a formal psychological evaluation confirmed this strong suspicion. Ever since, he has endeavored to identify and tease apart common communication glitches that can be so destructive in relationships.

Bob, an NLP Practitioner, is an est graduate (1975) and has gone through The Landmark Education Forum two additional times (1997 and 2006) in conjunction with Landmark's 10-week "Communications Workshop."

Made in the USA
San Bernardino,
CA